RAPE
AND RAPE-RELATED ISSUES

GARLAND REFERENCE LIBRARY
OF SOCIAL SCIENCE
(VOL. 39)

RAPE
AND RAPE-RELATED ISSUES
An Annotated Bibliography

Elizabeth Jane Kemmer

GARLAND PUBLISHING, INC. • NEW YORK & LONDON
1977

Library of Congress Cataloging in Publication Data

Kemmer, Elizabeth Jane.
    Rape and rape-related issues.

    (Garland reference library of social science ;
v. 39)
    Includes index.
    1.   Rape--United States--Bibliography.
I.   Title.
Z7164.S44K45   [HV6561]   016.3641'53   76-52701
ISBN 0-8240-9873-0

To all victims of rape, with the hope that this bibliography may, in some way, lead to an increased understanding of the crime and its victims

CONTENTS

ACKNOWLEDGMENTS

Many people have contributed to the development of this book. I am extremely grateful to Carol Trilling for her constant availability and eagerness to help with all phases of this project; her advice and suggestions were invaluable. I would also like to thank Jack M. Kress for sharing his expertise in the areas of the law and the criminal justice system, Shelle Preston for her advice concerning the technical points of compiling bibliographies, and the staff of the Interlibrary Loan Office of the State University of New York at Albany Library for procuring much of the material in this bibliography. Carole Ann, Barbara, Pat, Carol, Lisa Anne, Valerie, Joanne, Joe, Diane, and Dorothy also contributed much by their enthusiasm and encouragement. Finally, I owe special thanks to Wendy Kwalwasser, whose persistent encouragement made this bibliography possible.

INTRODUCTION

Rape is the most rapidly increasing and misunderstood violent crime in America. It is estimated that only about one in every ten rapes is reported, and of the very few that are reported, only a small number result in convictions. In examining the literature written on the subject of rape over a ten-year period, certain patterns emerge that may explain this paradox.

Discussions of the legal process in regard to rape inevitably focus on the operations of the criminal justice system. When a rape victim reports the crime to the police, she is often met with incredulous remarks and unsympathetic attitudes. Because of the nature of rape statutes in many states, the trial becomes a kind of nightmare for the victim, in which the defendant is treated as the victim of a false charge, and responsibility for the crime is attributed to the rape victim. Consequently, many rapists are never convicted of rape.

A sexual-assault victim seeking medical help may encounter similar responses from medical personnel. Rape victims have experienced longer-than-average waits in hospital emergency rooms, and their physical, emotional, and psychological needs have often been inadequately served because of the shortage of specialized personnel to deal with rape cases.

The attitudes of police, court personnel, medical personnel, and the public toward rape may be attributed to the many myths concerning the crime and to the process of sex-role socialization, which is initiated during childhood. Prevalent myths and sex-role stereotypes are perpetuated through the media, thus legitimizing the popular conceptions of the sexually aggressive male and the weak, passive female and, in so doing, providing justifications for rape.

In examining the rape literature chronologically, a definite trend can be observed. Prior to 1965, very little was written on the subject of rape. From approximately 1965 to 1968, rape literature focused on the offender and the unjust system that convicted the falsely accused male of so heinous a crime. The sympathy of the public was with the offender, thus making the victim the guilty party in a rape situation. This attitude is reflected in statistics and literature concerning the incidence of rape, in rape reporting, and in rape convictions for the years mentioned. Rape was still a fairly silent, secret crime—a crime whose victims were the most silent of all.

In 1968, the Women's Liberation Movement and the revival of feminism brought a new perspective to the problem of rape. Women began to look at themselves as people and to scrutinize their positions in society and in relationships with others. Women became angry enough to initiate action to stop the injustices they saw and to give themselves the freedom that they desired. During this revolutionary period (and continuing through to the present), there was a noticeable shift in the focus of rape literature. The victim was now the recipient of sympathy and the object of legislative and societal reform. The women's movement has provided the impetus necessary to gain increased rights for rape victims through legislative reform, public education programs, improved methods for hospital personnel in treating sexual-assault victims, empathic counseling programs, rape-crisis centers, and self-defense classes.

Yet rape remains a heinous offense that does not receive the attention that it deserves, and rape victims are still treated unjustly by the public and the criminal justice system. The media continue to glorify and romanticize violent sexual behavior, and more rapists go free than are convicted of the offense. The incidence of rape continues to rise, and women still live in fear of the crime.

Despite current reforms, rape is still very much a concern of most women in this country. Until societal attitudes toward the crime and its victims change, women will continue to be victimized and rape will persist as the most rapidly increasing and misunderstood violent crime in America.

This bibliography includes literature on rape published in English from 1965 through the summer of 1976. The bibliography is arranged alphabetically by author; in cases where no author is stated, the entry is alphabetized according to the first significant word in the title. A listing of all periodical literature represented follows the bibliography.

The subject index is concise, focusing on those subjects that reflect important issues of concern in the area of rape. Please note that reference numbers refer to the number of the abstract and not to the number of the page on which the abstract may be found.

1. Abel, Gene G., and others. "Psychological Treatment
   of Rapists." in: Walker, Marcia J. and Stanley
   L. Brodsky, editors, SEXUAL ASSAULT. Lexington,
   Massachusetts: Lexington Books, 1976, pp. 99-115.

   The authors discuss the psychological treatment
   of sex offenders and examine its effectiveness.
   Methods for evaluating treatment programs are
   explored, including the empathic relationship
   between the offender and the therapist. The
   process of finding a totally effective treatment
   program for rapists is hindered by the lack of
   acessibility of offenders for treatment and study.
   A diversity of methods and lengths of treatment
   also hinders the evaluation of treatment programs.
   A table containing the results of treatment at
   various centers accross the country is included.

2. "Age No Barrier to Rape." PRIME TIME, September 1974,
   p. 3.

   The author of this artice, a woman in her late
   fifties, had been the victim of a rape. She
   describes her experiences in dealing with the
   police and emergency room personnel immediately
   following the assault, emphasizing her psychological
   reactions to these encounters, and to the rape
   itself.

3. Aitken, Janet. "Rape Prosecutions." WOMEN LAWYERS
   JOURNAL, 60: 197-203, Fall 1974.

   Rape is defined according to the California Penal
   Code and catagories of rapists and rape victims
   are explained. The author discusses in detail the
   rape investigation, the trial, and the final charge
   and instructions of the judge to the jury. Reform
   in legislation concerning the initial interview of
   the rape victim and the pre-trial and trial
   procedures is suggested.

4. Alexander, Shana. "A Simple Question of rape."
   NEWSWEEK, 84(18): 110, October 28, 1974.

   Rape is defined in a variety of ways by different
   segments of the society. This diversity of definitions
   is discussed and the various myths concerning rape,
   which have been passed down through history, are
   explored. Alexander focuses on the trial of Inez
   Garcia, a rape victim who had shot and killed one

of her assailants. In her concluding remarks,
the author states that Garcia is an example of
"a woman suffering from both a patriarchal
crime snd patriarchal justice" as well as being
a victim of feminist attitudes.

5. American College of Obstetricians and Gynecologists.
    "Suspected Rape." ACOG TECHNICAL BULLETIN,
    Number 14, July 1970.

    This bulletin outlines the procedures to be
    followed by physicians in handling suspected
    rape cases. Rape, statutory rape, and sexual
    molestation are defined, and precautions to
    be observed by the physician in protecting
    himself and his patient are suggested. Detailed
    procedures for the physicial examination of
    the victim, the collecting of specimens for
    laboratory analysis, retention of clothing and
    other evidence, and the recording of statements
    made by the victim during the examination are
    discussed. This bulletin also provides methods
    to be employed by the physician to prevent the
    pregnancy and venereal disease which may occur
    as a result of the rape.

6. Amir, Menachem. "Forcible Rape." FEDERAL PROBATION,
    31(1): 51-58, March 1967.

    This article is based on a study conducted by
    the author in Philadelphia, Pennsylvania. The
    subjects of his study were 646 cases of forcible
    rape occurring in this city over two twelve
    month periods, one year apart. The data was
    collected from police files. The author devotes
    this article to an explanation of the findings
    of this study. The following variables are
    discussed: race, age, marital status, occupation,
    time and place of the offense, previous criminal
    record of the offender and the victim, the
    degree of violence displayed in the assault,
    victim-offender relationship, and the use of
    alcohol in connection with the rape. Multiple
    rapes, felony rapes, and victim precipitated
    rapes are also discussed in detail. Amir
    concludes that a subculture of violence theory
    is appropriate to explain the findings of this
    study, and that more studies of this kind are
    necessary to an understanding of the problem
    of rape.

7. Amir, Menachem. "Forcible Rape." SEXUAL BEHAVIOR,
        1(8): 25-36, November 1971.

    The sociological and psychological aspects
    of forcible rape are explored. Topics discussed
    include: the relationship between the victim
    and the offender, the setting of the crime, the
    planning and execution of the rape by the
    offender, methods employed in committing the
    offense, rape by multiple offenders, and
    general characteristics of offenders. Amir
    uses statistics from his own study of forcible
    rape in Philadelphia, Pennsylvania to illustrate
    each topic. Socioeconomic factors contributing
    to the development of aggressive sexual behavior
    and the growth of lower class subcultures are
    also discussed. The article concludes with
    answers to some frequently asked questions
    concerning rape.

8. Amir, Menachem. PATTERNS IN FORCIBLE RAPE.
        Chicago: University of Chicago Press, 1971.
        394 pages.

    This work is primarily a sociological and
    scientific study of forcible rape in the city
    of Philadelphia, Pennsylvania for the years of
    1958 and 1960. Socioeconomic, racial, temporal,
    and spatial factors are considered in Amir's
    analysis, along with the effect of alcohol upon
    the assault, the previous criminal record of
    the victim and/or the offender, and the
    relationship between the offender and the victim.
    Amir also discusses rape as a victim precipitated
    crime, and finds that in nineteen percent (19%)
    of the rapes studied, very few showed evidence
    of victim precipitation. The data used in
    this study is analyzed in detail, and definite
    patterns are identified. The orientation of
    the work is empirical and sociological.
    Comparisons and contrasts with respect to
    rape and race, age of victim and offender,
    social and economic background, marital status,
    and other related factors are also made where
    relevant.

    This work includes a thirty page bibliography.

9. Amir, Menachem. "Victim Precipitated Forcible Rape."
   THE JOURNAL OF CRIMINAL LAW, CRIMINOLOGY, AND
   POLICE SCIENCE, 58(4): 493-502, 1967.

   The author states that precipitation must be
   differentiated from provocation. In the case
   of rape, precipitation means that the offender
   interprets the victim's behavior as consenting
   or inviting. The victim may give this impression
   by something she does (for example, accepting a
   ride with a stranger) or by something she fails
   to do (for example, reacting strongly against
   suggestions of sexual activity). Amir discusses
   victim precipitation in cases of forcible rape
   with the use of data collected in Phildelphia,
   Pennsylvania. Race, age, presence of alcohol,
   location of the initial meeting between the
   offender and the victim, location of the
   crime, the use of violence, and victim-offender
   relationships are among the topics discussed.
   Analysis of the data revealed certain demographic
   and behavioral patterns which Amir describes
   in detail.

10. Andrea, Alice Sant. "New Rights for Rape Victims."
    MAJORITY REPORT, 4(20): 9, February 8, 1975.

    Amendments to the rape statutes in various
    states are discussed. The significance of
    these amendments for the victim is emphasized,
    and the sexist character which has traditionally
    overshadowed rape laws is discussed. The
    Michigan Criminal Code with respect to rape
    is explored in detail as an example of a law
    which encourages victims of rape to report the
    crime and to prosecute their assailants.

11. Arnold, Peter. LADY BEWARE. Garden City, New York:
    Doubleday and Company, Inc., 1974. 183 pages.

    Arnold suggests ways of preventing property
    crimes as well as violent personal crimes such
    as rape. Ways of securing one's home, apartment,
    and car against intrusion are presented, in
    addition to tips for protecting one's person
    while walking or hitchhiking. Crimes occurring
    between family members, and ways of preventing
    them, are also discussed. The author concludes
    his book with a warning that every woman is a
    potential victim of crime. To prevent crime,

a person must be alert to the possibility
that she may, at some time, be a victim of
a crime, and act defensively by taking
precautions for preventing it from occurring.

12. Astor,Gerald. THE CHARGE IS RAPE. New York:
    Playboy Press, 1974. 215 pages.

    The problem of rape is discussed primarily
    from the victim's perspective. Victims relate
    their experiences and the effect of the crime
    on their lives. The history of rape and rape
    legislation is explored, and some famous rape
    cases are examined. Law enforcement officials
    explain procedures for investigating rape
    complaints and the problems encountered during
    an investigation. The author concludes with
    some suggestions for treatment and increased
    understanding of the crime of rape and its
    victims.

13. Astor, Gerald. A QUESTION OF RAPE. New York:
    Pinnacle Books, 1974. 254 pages.

    The issue of interracial rape has always
    been an explosive one. A QUESTION OF RAPE
    is the story of an interracial rape, based
    on an actual case, in which two black men
    are accused of raping a sixteen year old white
    woman in the state of Maryland. The men,
    falsely accused of the rape, were tried for
    the crime, found guilty, and were sentenced
    to death according to Maryland law. Astor
    carries his reader through the entire case,
    beginning with the accusation and ending,
    years after the sentencing, with a pardon
    by the court. The issue of a fair trial by
    a jury of one's peers is central to this
    book. The defendants in this case were black,
    and the jurors were all white. The defense
    attorneys were appointed by the court, and
    the defense was ineffectual. Since there
    was little substantial evidence to support
    the charge of rape, the author implies that
    the conviction was based on racial bias
    rather than evidence.

14. Bailey, F. Lee and Henry B. Rosenblatt. CRIMES
    OF VIOLENCE: RAPE AND OTHER SEX CRIMES.
    Rochester, New York: The Lawyers Cooperative
    Publishing Company, 1973. 385 pages.

    This book is written primarily for attorneys
    and deals, in large part, with questions
    concerning the defense of persons accused
    of committing sex crimes. In addition to
    violent sex crimes, the authors discuss
    so-called "victimless crimes" such as
    prostitution and homosexuality. Most of
    the discussion of the offenses themselves
    is somewhat superficial, the emphasis of
    the work being on the defense of the criminal
    case, and the issues surrounding it, for
    both attorney and defendant. Topics such
    as what fee the attorney should charge for
    services, plea bargaining, and confessions
    are discussed.

15. Barber, Ross. "Judge and Jury Attitudes to Rape."
    AUSTRALIAN AND NEW ZEALAND JOURNAL OF
    CRIMINOLOGY, 7(3): 157-172, September 1974.

    The results of an investigation conducted
    by the author into the attitudes of the
    judges and juries involved in rape cases
    in Queensland, over a ten year period, are
    presented. The effect of offender, victim,
    and situational characteristics upon the
    severity of sentencing, and upon jury decisions,
    are explored in detail, with the assistance
    of the Chi-square test to determine the
    statistical significance of correlations
    between the variables studied. Barber found
    that the only factor affecting both the
    sentencing decisions of the judges and
    the verdicts of the juries was the moral
    character of the victim.

16. Bard, Morton. "The Rape Victim: Challenge to the
    Helping Systems." VICTIMOLOGY: AN
    INTERNATIONAL JOURNAL, 1(2): 263-271,
    Summer 1976.

    The findings of recent research on rape are
    explored, identifying factors common to a
    majority of the studies. The victim's

psychological reactions to the assault were
central to these studies and are discussed
in detail. Bard identifies the helping
systems, or human service agencies, which
play important roles in the treatment of
rape victims. The most vital systems--
health care facilities, police, social and
mental health agencies, and women's support
groups--are discussed. Bard recognizes the
importance of developing specific strategies
for change in the area of care for the rape
victim, and suggests methods for coordinating
programs for change within organizations.
He states that the victim should be the prime
determinant of need when considering
particular programs for planned change.

17. Bard, Morton and Katherine Ellison. "Crisis
     Intervention and Investigation of Forcible
     Rape." THE POLICE CHIEF, 41(5): 68-74,
     May 1974.

     Crisis situations, stress, and reactions
     to stress are discussed in detail. The role
     of the police as crisis intervention agents
     is explored, emphasizing the impact of the
     officer's immediacy and authority upon the
     crisis situation. The crime of rape is also
     discussed and the case history of a rape
     is presented. The authors conclude by
     stressing the significance of an understanding
     of crisis situations and crisis intervention
     on the part of police investigators in rape
     cases, and the impact of this understanding
     upon the victim and the investigation.

18. Baril, Cecile and Iain S. B. Couchman. "Legal
     Rights." SOCIETY, 13: 15-17, July/August
     1976.

     Rape laws are interpreted from a feminist
     perspective. The authors state that rape
     laws perpetuate stereotypic images of male
     and female roles, which reinforce the image
     of woman as a sex object rather than as a
     person. A rape victim's civil and legal
     rights are not respected by the legal
     system, since the court process in a rape
     case tends to transfer guilt to the victim
     by doubting her credibility. This article

7

contrasts rape laws with laws governing
other forms of assaultive behavior. The
repeal of rape laws as special catagories
of assault, and its effect on societal and
legal attitudes toward the crime, are
explored. The authors advocate the repeal
of rape laws. They state that by repealing
existing rape laws, the sexual aspect of
the crime will lose its importance, thus
promoting the victim's personal rights.

19. Barnes, Josephine. "Rape and Other Sexual
    Offenses." BRITISH MEDICAL JOURNAL,
    2: 293-295, April 29, 1967.

    The medical examination of a rape victim
    and the subsequent compilation of a medical
    report are explained. Barnes also explores
    the legal definitions of rape, incest,
    indecent assault, and other sexual offenses
    as defined by British law, and outlines
    procedures for conducting a medical examination
    of the victim of a sexual offense other than
    forcible rape.

20. Bassuk, Ellen and others. "Organizing a Rape
    Crisis Program in a General Hospital."
    JOURNAL OF THE AMERICAN MEDICAL WOMEN'S
    ASSOCIATION, 30(12): 486-490, December 1975.

    The development and organization of a rape
    crisis program at Beth Israel Hospital in
    Boston, Massachusetts is discussed in detail.
    The authors begin by stating that the crime
    of rape and its victims are frequently
    misunderstood, and that treatment programs
    for victims have been poorly organized and
    insensitively administered. The organizers
    of the Beth Israel crisis intervention program
    began by determining the needs of victims
    and subsequently designed a program based
    on those needs. In order to educate
    themselves and the general public to the
    crime of rape and the needs of rape victims,
    the counselors developed a program of
    research and public education.

21. Baughman, Laurence A. SOUTHERN RAPE COMPLEX:
    HUNDRED YEAR PSYCHOSIS. Atlanta, Georgia:
    Pendulum Books, 1966. 222 pages.

    Baughman discusses the phenomenon which is
    termed the "Southern Rape Complex" from an
    historical perspective. Central to the
    development of this "complex" is the idea
    of the southern woman as the property of
    her husband or her father. Also important
    to the existence of the "Southern Rape
    Complex" is the southern gentleman's loyalty
    to the South, and to the honor of the
    southern aristocracy. Symbolic and imagined
    rapes of white southern women by black men
    are discussed, in addition to actual and
    attempted rapes. Justifications for the
    existence of the "Southern Rape Complex"
    are also presented.

    This work includes a four page bibliography.

22. Bedau, Hugo Adam. "Felony Murder Rape and the
    Mandatory Death Penalty: A Study in
    Discretionary Justice." SUFFOLK UNIVERSITY
    LAW REVIEW, 10(3): 493-520, Spring 1976.

    Massachusetts law requires a mandatory death
    sentence for persons convicted of a homicide
    resulting from rape. This article explores
    the question of the mandatory death penalty
    for cases of murder resulting from rape,
    and the exercising of discretion in the
    disposition of such cases. The author
    obtained data from a study of first degree
    murder indictments in the two largest
    counties in Massachusetts. For this particular
    article, seventeen cases are summarized.
    Bedau found a discrepancy between the
    indictments, convictions, and sentences
    proscribed as mandatory for these offenses,
    and those actually handed down by the courts.

23. BenDor, Jan. "Justice After Rape: Legal Reform
    in Michigan." In: Walker, Marcia J. and
    Stanley L. Brodsky, SEXUAL ASSAULT.
    Lexington, Massachusetts: Lexington Books,
    1976, pp. 149-160.

    BenDor discusses Michigan's Criminal Sexual
    Conduct Law, which significantly changed

Michigan's existing rape laws. Law reform as an aid to eradicating rape is also discussed. The Criminal Sexual Conduct Law is contrasted with Michigan's prior rape law in detail, and implications for deterrence are mentioned. The author suggests that the passage of the Michigan law has led to the enactment of similar legislation in other states.

24. Betries, Joyce. "Rape: An Act of Possession." SWEET FIRE, 23: 12, Summer 1972.

Following an account of her own experience with rape, the author discusses reasons why most women do not choose to report rape. The remainder of this article discusses the politics of rape from an historical perspective, focusing on the racial and sexist bias of society and of the legal system. Betries concludes with a powerful comparison of attitudes toward rape in the United States and in non-capitalist countries, stating that the non-capitalist countries treat women with respect and not as possessions to be exploited, and that rape is considered to be"a crime against the people."

25. Billings, Victoria. "How to Tell If You're Being Raped--And What to Do About It." REDBOOK MAGAZINE, 144(1): 70-74, November 1974.

Not all rapes are forcible rapes as defined by law. Following a brief discussion of forcible rape, the author discusses another form of rape--petty rape-- which is not accomplished with physical force. A petty rape is one in which the victim is pressured or coerced, perhaps subtly, into sexual relations. In this instance, the woman is playing the role of victim by submitting to something she may not want. Billings suggests that the best defense against petty rape is "self respect, an understanding of the social psychology of rape, and self-assertion--a woman must be capable . . . of saying 'no'." She also states that a woman is not required to justify her decision

not to have sexual relations, and if sex
is considered an obligation, there is really
no freedom of choice. When a woman agrees
to sexual relations out of guilt or feelings
of obligation, she becomes a victim of
petty rape.

26. Blaise, Madelaine. "Haunting Memories Are an
    Aftermath of Rape Experience." BOSTON
    SUNDAY GLOBE, December 3, 1972, pg. 17.

    A rape experience leaves the victim with
    feelings of isolation, powerlessness, and
    loss of human dignity. Blaise relates such
    an experience, in which the victim, after
    being raped in her own apartment, decided
    to report the crime to the police and to
    seek medical attention for her injuries.
    The victim's experiences with police and
    hospital personnel, which were generally
    positive, are discussed. The author
    concludes this article by quoting the
    victim, whose feelings reflect those of
    many victims of sexual assault: "In this
    country, property is more important than
    human life. . . . Women are forced to bear
    the responsibility for male aggression."

27. Blitman, Nan and Robin Green. "Inez Garcia on
    Trial." MS. MAGAZINE, 3(11): 49-54 and
    84-88, May 1975.

    The rape and trial of Inez Garcia is
    discussed in detail. Garcia was convicted
    of first degree murder for killing one of
    the men who had raped her. The authors
    point out that the rape was treated by the
    court as a virtually irrelevant incident,
    even though the rape was Garcia's motive for
    committing the murder. Garcia's emotional
    state immediately following the rape was
    also considered to be immaterial. The
    authors quote one of the jurors, a young
    woman, who stated that if the shooting had
    occurred during the rape itself, "there
    would have been no problem. But because
    she went looking for them. . . ." Thus,
    this article implies that the issue of a
    woman's right to react to man's violence

11

with violence was an issue in the Garcia
trial, and it seemed to be more than just
an incident of a rape victim fighting back
against her assailant.

28. Bohmer, Carol. "Judicial Attitudes Toward Rape
Victims." JUDICATURE, 57(7): 303-307,
February 1974.

Central to this article is what the author
terms the "courtroom victimization" of the
rape victim. Her assumption is that judicial
attitudes, especially the demeanor of the
judge, are determinants of judicial behavior,
and this has an effect on the victim's
experiences in the courtroom. Defenses
possible in rape cases, the legitimate victim,
the demeanor of the victim, and racial
attitudes of the judges are discussed. Bohmer
concludes by stating that the victim's
experience in the courtroom are important
to her adjustment to the aftermath of the
crime.

29. Bohmer, Carol. "Judicial Use of Psychiatric
Reports in the Sentencing of Sex Offenders."
JOURNAL OF PSYCHIATRY AND LAW, 1: 223-241,
Summer 1973.

The use of psychiatric reports in the pre-
sentence investigations of a sex offender
is frequently ordered by judges. This
article discusses these reports and their
value to judges in the sentencing of sex
offenders. Bohmer states that although the
judge may feel that these reports contain
information necessary to the sentencing
process, he may not be able to use the
reports due to constraints placed upon him
by the legal system and by other factors
which act to influence his decision.

30. Bohmer, Carol and Audrey Blumberg. "Twice
Traumatized: The Rape Victim and the Court."
JUDICATURE, 58(8): 391-399, March 1975.

The victim's role in the trial of a rape
case is central to this article. The authors
feel that the victim's role in the trial

is often misunderstood, since her primary
purpose is, officially, only to appear as
the state's primary witness in the trial.
Some problems involved in the court process
during a rape trial, including evidence and
societal factors which may act to influence
the jury's decision, and the impact of these
problems upon the victim are explored.
Bohmer and Blumberg conclude by pointing
out that the treatment of the victim and
the demeanor of law enforcement and court
personnel are, to a large extent, responsible
for the impact that the crime of rape
ultimately has on the victim, and the
difficulty or ease with which she adjusts
to her life after the assault.

31. Boston Women's Health Book Collective.
        "Defending Yourself Against Rape." LADIES
        HOME JOURNAL, 90(7): 62-68, 1973.
        also in: Boston Women's Health Book Collective,
        OUR BODIES, OURSELVES. New York: Simon and
        Schuster, Inc., 1973, p. 92.

        The authors state that if rape is going to
        be stopped, women must do it. Continuing
        in this vein, methods for preventing rape
        are suggested. The authors also discuss
        procedures to be followed in the event that
        a rape does occur.

32. Bowman, Karl M. and Bernice Engle. "Sexual
        Psychopath Laws." in: Slovenko, Ralph,
        editor, SEXUAL BEHAVIOR AND THE LAW.
        Springfield, Illinois: Charles C. Thomas,
        Publisher, 1965, pp. 757-778.

        The authors examine the development and
        application of sexual psychopath laws in
        the United States, providing examples from
        the statutes of various states. Statistics
        concerning the treatment of the sexual
        psychopath are provided. Some objections,
        both medical and legal, are raised concerning
        the diagnosis of a person as a sexual
        psychopath, and his subsequent hearing and
        committment. It is suggested that these
        proceedings violate the defendant's civil
        rights, and that the proceedings and the
        laws identifying and diagnosing persons
        as sexual psychopaths be revised.

33. Brabec, Bette Dewing. "Rape: The Ultimate
    Violence." PRIME TIME, September 1974,
    p. 7.

    Brabec feels that the crime of rape is not
    given the proper consideration and attention
    it deserves from the media, the legislatures,
    law enforcement personnel, and the court
    system. In addition to some suggestions
    for avoiding rape, situations which are
    particularly condusive to rape are
    presented. The influence of sexual
    violence in films, television, magazines,
    and books on the increasing rate of rape
    and other violent crimes is also discussed.

34. Breen, James L. and others. "The Molested Young
    Female: Evaluation and Therapy of Alleged
    Rape." PEDIATRIC CLINICS OF NORTH AMERICA,
    19(3): 717-725, August 1972.

    The authors discuss procedures involved in
    the medical examination of a victim of an
    alleged rape. Precautions taken to prevent
    disease and pregnancy are summarized. The
    collecting of medical evidence for the court
    is also discussed, including the victim's
    statements concerning the assault and a
    description of her assailant.

35. Brodsky, Carroll M. "Rape At Work." in: Walker,
    Marcia J. and Stanley L. Brodsky, editors,
    SEXUAL ASSAULT. Lexington, Massachusetts:
    Lexington Books, 1976, pp. 35-51.

    Rape which occurs at a woman's place of
    employment is discussed with the use of case
    studies. Rape which occurs at work may have
    a different effect on a woman than a rape
    which occurs in a different setting, such
    as a park or a street. Brodsky feels that
    the impact of a rape occurring at work is
    more devastating than one which occurs in
    an unfamiliar place, and the victim's
    ability to do her job in the future may be
    impaired. Ways of counseling the victim
    are discussed, including finding her a job
    where she will feel less vulnerable to rape.

14

36. Brodsky, Stanley L. "Prevention of Rape:
    Deterrence By the Potential Victim."
    in: Walker, Marcia J. and Stanley L.
    Brodsky, editors, SEXUAL ASSAULT.
    Lexington, Massachusetts: Lexington
    Books, 1976, pp. 75-90.

    Brodsky studied the effect of verbal
    responses of potential victims to rapists
    as possible deterrents for rape. Through
    the use of videotapes, various responses
    of victims were studied and rated by
    professionals working in the area of rape.
    The responses were rated according to their
    effectiveness in deterring a potential
    rapist. The author also asked rapists to
    view the videotapes and to rate the victims'
    responses as possible deterrents. They
    were also asked what efforts by the victims
    would have been effective in preventing
    the crime that they themselves had committed.
    The rapists then suggested methods for
    deterring the potential rapist. Brodsky
    emphasizes that the effectiveness of a
    deterrent depends upon the character of
    the individual rapist, and the circumstances
    surrounding the potential assault.

37. Brodsky, Stanley L. "Sexual Assault: Perspectives
    on Prevention and Assailants." in: Walker,
    Marcia J. and Stanley L. Brodsky, editors,
    SEXUAL ASSAULT. Lexington, Massachusetts:
    Lexington Books, 1976, pp. 1-7.

    This article focuses on rape prevention.
    Brodsky examines attributions of blame for
    sexual assault to the victim, and to the
    offender, and discusses prevention in the
    context of this examination. Society is
    also examined as a focus of blame, as is
    the situation in which the rape occurs.
    The author stresses the importance of
    departing from conventional methods of
    rape prevention, as they often do not
    reflect the realities of the situations
    dealt with. He suggests methods of prevention
    which would resocialize the public, to a
    certain extent, by changing their outmoded
    and untrue conceptions of rape, and of the

roles of men and women in sexual encounters. Technological devices, such as alarms, are also recommended as methods of rape prevention. Brodsky concludes by stating that by blaming the assailant alone for a sexual assault is far too simplistic, and a much better explanation for causation is needed.

38. Brown, William P. "Police-Victim Relationships in Sex Crime Investigations." THE POLICE CHIEF, 37(1): 20-24, January 1970.

Police personnel frequently encounter difficulties when dealing with the victims of sex crimes. Brown discusses the two main groups of sexual assault victims-- female children and adult women--focusing on the particular needs of each immediately following the assault. The importance of the victim's relationship with the police is emphasized. The author states that a good relationship between the police and the victim not only helps the victim to adjust to her life immediately following the assault, but also assists the police in conducting a better and more thorough investigation of the crime. Guidelines for improving the relationship between the police and the victim of a sexual offense are suggested.

39. Brownmiller, Susan. AGAINST OUR WILL: MEN, WOMEN, AND RAPE. New York: Simon and Schuster, 1975. 472 pages.

Brownmiller provides a political, historical, and sociological analysis of rape. The history of rape and rape laws, rape during periods of war, rape and sexual abuse of children, and the psychological trauma of the rape victim's experience are only a few of the topics discussed. Many of the myths which have been used as justifications for rape throughout history are scrutinized. Feminist issues such as the powerlessness of women and forced female submission to the male dominated culture are discussed. Brownmiller also suggests methods for

decreasing or eradicating rape through
methods such as the reform of rape
legislation and improved means for
determining appropriate punishment or
treatment for sex offenders.

40. Brownmiller, Susan. "Anti-Rape Technique."
    HARPER'S BAZAAR, 109(3172): 119-136,
    March 1976.

    Methods for preventing rape are suggested.
    Brownmiller states that a woman must learn
    to recognize the warning signals of pre-
    rape situations, and to react defensively.
    Frequently, the use of physical strength
    by a potential rape victim is useless
    because the victim may not be strong
    enough to successfully defend herself
    against her assailant. The author
    advocates the use of one's "wits" instead
    of attempting to resist or deter her
    assailant with a strength that may not be
    effective, and may result in more harm than
    good. The entire situation must be considered
    in deciding what preventive measures may
    be effective in a particular rape situation.

41. Brussel, James A. "The Menaced Woman May Suffer
    More Than the Beaten One." SEXUAL
    BEHAVIOR, 1(8): 30, November 1971.

    Commenting on Menachem Amir's article,
    "Forcible Rape," appearing in this issue
    of SEXUAL BEHAVIOR, Brussel discusses some
    problems with the laws concerning rape.
    The definition of rape by law may differ
    from the definition used by psychiatrists
    and psychologists who are frequently asked
    to testify at rape trials. Also, the
    definition of force is sometimes unclear,
    and the victim subjected to physical force
    may suffer less emotional and psychological
    trauma than the victim who submits out of
    fear for her life. The author states that
    all rape cases should not be treated alike,
    since the personalities and backgrounds of
    the offenders and victims are not alike in
    every case, and the definitions of different
    types of motivations for the crime are
    often unclear.

42. Burgess, Ann Wolbert and Lynda Lytle Holstrom. "Coping Behavior of the Rape Victim." AMERICAN JOURNAL OF PSYCHIATRY, 133(4): 413-417, April 1976.

   The means employed by rape victims to cope with their lives immediately following the assault may vary greatly from individual to individual. The authors state, however, that, generally, a victim's coping behavior will pass through three phases. These phases are described, along with various coping strategies within each general phase. In counseling the rape victim, it is necessary to understand that each victim has her own form of coping behavior. The recognition of this fact enables the counselor to provide support for the victim and to develop the additional counseling techniques needed to aid the victim in her efforts to adapt to present and future crisis situations, which may occur as a result of the rape.

43. Burgess, Ann Wolbert and Lynda Lytle Holmstrom. "Crisis and Counseling Requests of Rape Victims." NURSING RESEARCH, 23(3): 196-202, May-June 1974.

   The authors studied one hundred forty-six (146) adult and child victims of sexual assaults. The subjects were interviewed at the hospital immediately following the assaults, and follow-up studies were also conducted. Specific requests of the victims during the crisis period immediately following the assault were identified as medical attention, police intervention, and psychological counseling. During the follow-up interviews, the victims' needs changed, and emphasis was placed on emotional and supportive services. The specific counseling requests of the victims, considered to be important factors in the negotiation of a relationship between client and counselor, are also presented.

44. Burgess, Ann Wolbert and Lynda Lytle Holmstrom.
    "Rape: Its Effect on Task Performance at
    Varying Stages in the Life Cycle."
    in: Walker, Marcia J. and Stanley L.
    Brodsky, editors, SEXUAL ASSAULT.
    Lexington, Massachusetts: Lexington Books,
    1976, pp. 23-33.

    The authors find that rape has a tremendous
    effect on every aspect of the victim's
    life, including her ability to perform
    expected tasks. Task disruptions of adults
    and of children are examined. The
    problems encountered in counseling the
    victims are discussed, and suggestions
    for improvements in counseling procedures
    are proposed. Recommendations are made
    to assist the victim in coping with the
    aftermath of the rape.

45. Burgess, Ann Wolbert and Lynda Lytle Holmstrom.
    RAPE: VICTIMS OF CRISIS. Bowie, Maryland:
    Robert J. Brady Company, 1974. 308 pages.

    Rape is discussed from both the victim's
    and the rapist's points of view. A large
    portion of this book deals with counseling
    the rape victim, and draws on the
    counseling experiences of the authors.
    Prostitution, the child victim, and the
    male victim of homosexual rape are among
    the topics discussed. The reactions of
    various social institutions to the problem
    of rape are presented, along with examples
    of community based treatment and counseling
    programs established to assist the rape
    victim.

    The authors include an eleven page glossary
    of terms used throughout the book.

46. Burgess, Ann Wolbert and Lynda Lytle Holmstrom.
    "Rape Trauma Syndrome." AMERICAN JOURNAL
    OF PSYCHIATRY, 131(9): 981-986, September
    1974.

    Upon interviewing rape victims in the
    emergency ward of a city hospital, the
    authors were able to identify the presence
    of a rape trauma syndrome. In this article,

19

the syndrome is described and its symptoms
are discussed. Three different types of
reactions are identified, and the treatment
techniques employed for each type are
presented. The authors believe that the
woman's need for self-preservation,
emotional as well as physical, is important
to the treatment process. With this as a
goal to keep in mind, the victim is better
able to respond to treatment and adapt to
her particular life style.

47. Burgess, Ann Wolbert and Lynda Lytle Holmstrom.
    "The Rape Victim in the Emergency Ward."
    AMERICAN JOURNAL OF NURSING, 73(10):
    1741-1745, October 1973.

    A victim counseling program was developed
    at the Boston City Hospital in order to
    provide needed support services to rape
    victims. The organization and operation
    of this program are described in detail,
    and the psychological and social
    consequences of rape for the victim are
    explored. The authors discuss the
    victims' responses to questions about the
    crime and draw inferences about the
    psychological impact of the rape on the
    victim from these responses.

48. Bush, Mary. "Sex Offenders Are People!"
    JOURNAL OF PSYCHIATRIC NURSING AND
    MENTAL HEALTH SERVICES, 13: 38-40,
    July-August 1975.

    The author, a nurse and instructor of
    psychosocial nursing, discusses her
    experiences in working with a sex offender
    treatment program at Western State
    Hospital in Fort Steilacoom, Washington.
    The structure and operation of the program
    is presented, and the role of the
    psychiatric nurse in forensic psychiatry
    is discussed.

49. Butler, Donald P. "The Imposition of the Death
    Penalty for Rape Where the Victim's Life
    Has Been Neither Taken Nor Endangered
    Constitutes Cruel and Unusual Punishment
    Under the Eighth Amendment." HOUSTON
    LAW REVIEW, 8(4): 795-807, March 1971.

    This selection begins with an historical
    look at the principle of cruel and unusual
    punishment. Through the use of examples
    drawn from actual cases, Butler discusses
    this principle in relation to the crime
    of rape in Maryland, where the death
    penalty has been applied for rape. In
    cases where the victim's life is not
    endangered, the death penalty is felt
    to be disproportional to the offense, and
    thus in violation of the eighth amendment's
    proscription against cruel and unusual
    punishment. In conclusion, Butler states
    that in cases where the death penalty is
    not proportional with the offense, there
    is a denial of due process and equal
    protection, which are also guarenteed
    by the United States Constitution.

50. Calvert, Catherine. "Is Rape What Women Really
    Want?" MADEMOISELLE, 78(5): 134-137,
    March 1974.

    Calvert explodes the myth that proclaims
    every woman's secret desire to be raped.
    She stresses the impact of the media in
    promulgating this myth: Man uses rape
    to prove his masculinity and exercise his
    superiority, and woman is punished by
    society and the law for being passive
    and vulnerable in the rape situation.
    After presenting a history of attitudes
    toward rape and rape victims, statistics
    on the incidence of rape in the United
    States, and victim and offender characteristics,
    the author discusses the operations of rape
    crisis centers, emphasizing their importance
    in providing supportive services for the
    victim.

51. Camps, Francis E. "The Christie Case." THE
    CRIMINOLOGIST, 5(16-17): 25-41, May-August
    1970.

    The investigations of the infamous Christie
    sex-murder cases in England are the subjects
    of this article by Camps, a doctor and
    investigator who assisted in the investigation
    of the Christie case. Camps begins with a
    brief account of Christie's activities just
    prior to the discovery of the bodies of his
    victims by the police. A very detailed
    description of the condition of these
    bodies follows, culminating in a criticism
    of the investigatory methods used by the
    police, pathologists, and others engaged
    in gathering and analyzing the evidence in
    the case.

52. Capraro, Vincent J. "Sexual Assault of Female
    Children." ANNALS OF THE NEW YORK ACADEMY
    OF SCIENCES, 142: 817-819, 1967.

    The focus of this article is on the
    treatment of the sexually assaulted female
    child. The importance of giving emotional
    support to the victim, in addition to
    specialized medical treatment, is
    emphasized. The procedure followed by
    medical personnel at a New York hospital
    is described in detail. Capraro mentions
    the necessity of cooperation between the
    police, the courts, and medical personnel
    in the treatment of the rape victim.

53. "Certification of Rape Under the Colorado
    Abortion Statute." UNIVERSITY OF COLORADO
    LAW REVIEW, 42(1): 121-128, May 1970.

    In Colorado, a pregnancy which is the
    result of a rape may be legally aborted,
    if the district attorney certifies that
    a rape had actually been committed. This
    article compares the Colorado procedure
    for verifying a rape with procedures
    followed in other states. The role of the
    district attorney in the verification
    procedure is discussed and recommendations
    to minimize the possibility of arbitrary
    decisions by the district attorney are
    suggested.

54. Chaneles, Sol. "Child Victims of Sex Offenses."
     FEDERAL PROBATION, 31(2): 52-56, June 1967.

     Based on a child victimization study
     conducted by the American Humane Association
     and directed by the author, this article
     discusses the problem of sexual abuse of
     children and suggests ways to prevent or
     control the crime. Chaneles states that
     sexual abuse of children is committed
     most frequently by persons known to the
     victim, or to the victim's family. The
     findings of this study show that in twenty
     percent (20%) of the cases studied, only
     five percent (5%) of the sex offenses
     against children were committed by total
     strangers. Procedures of the official
     agencies which deal with sexual victimization
     of children, the impact of the offense on
     the child, and the extent of the problem
     of sexual abuse of children are among the
     topics discussed.

55. Chappell, Duncan. "Forcible Rape and the
     Criminal Justice System: Surveying
     Present Practices and Projecting Future
     Trends." in: Walker, Marcia J. and
     Stanley L. Brodsky, editors, SEXUAL
     ASSAULT. Lexington, Massachusetts:
     Lexington Books, 1976, pp. 9-22.

     This selection discusses the activities of
     the criminal justice system which are
     directed at identifying areas of the
     system in need of change, and suggesting
     specific changes. Chappell describes in
     detail a research project designed with
     these goals in mind. The need for written
     guidelines for interviewing victims of
     violent crimes, specialized personnel to
     investigate rape cases, and a program of
     public education were recognized as a
     result of the research project. The
     existence of a diversity of definitions
     for rape and a diversity in the methods
     for reporting and recording rape cases are
     among the procedural problems identified
     and discussed by Chappell.

56. Chappell, Duncan, Gilbert Geis, and Faith Fogarty.
    "Forcible Rape: Bibliography." THE JOURNAL
    OF CRIMINAL LAW AND CRIMINOLOGY, 65(2):
    248-263, 1974.

    This bibliography lists articles and books
    written on the subject of forcible rape in
    the United States and in foreign countries,
    written in English and in other languages.
    The authors have divided the bibliography
    into sections which focus on the offender,
    the victim, the law, medical aspects of
    the crime, sociological aspects, and
    police investigation. A brief introduction
    to forcible rape is included.

57. Chappell, Duncan and others. "Forcible Rape:
    A Comparative Study of Offenses Known
    th the Police in Boston and Los Angeles."
    in: Henslin, James, editor, STUDIES IN
    THE SOCIOLOGY OF SEX. New York: Meredith,
    1971, 169-190.

    Following a comment as to the value of a
    comparative approach to the study of
    culture and law, the authors present
    anthropological evidence to support the
    theory that the incidence of rape, the
    methods employed in carrying out the
    offense, and the people involved in the
    act are all the results of the sexual and
    social climate in which the rape occurs.
    In analyzing the data on rape from Boston
    and Los Angeles, the authors examined the
    patterns of rape and the police processing
    of rape complaints in each city. Statistically
    significant differences between the two
    cities were found in regard to the time of
    the week and the season of the year in
    which the offenses occurred, the number of
    accomplices involved, the race of the
    offender, and the relationship between the
    offender and the victim. The authors
    conclude that the more permissive the city,
    the higher the incidence of rape in that
    city. Also, differences in police policies
    and procedures did not appear to
    significantly alter this trend.

58. Chase, Carl. "Rape and Police Professionalism."
       CAROLINA LAW, 24(3): 67-75, May-June 1974.

    This article begins with excerpts from an
    article appearing in a recent journal
    which suggested ways to prevent rape and
    to defend one's self against sexual attack.
    However, the focus of Chase's work is on
    police methods for dealing with rape cases,
    and emphasis is placed on the victim,
    including necessary medical and emotional
    care. Examples of forms use by the
    physician during the physical examination
    of the rape victim and the collecting of
    physical evidence are included. The author
    feels that by the police handling rape
    cases with a great degree of professionalism,
    victims will be encouraged to report the
    crime and prosecute their assailants.

59. Child, Barbara. "Ohio's New Rape Law: Does
       It Protect the Complainant at the Expense
       of the Rights of the Accused?" AKRON
       LAW REVIEW, 9(2): 337-359, Fall 1975.

    In an attempt to protect the victim of a
    sexual offense, the Ohio legislature enacted
    legislation revising the rape laws in Ohio.
    In providing background for the passage of
    the new law, Child discusses some
    traditional theories concerning the crime
    of rape and the effects of these theories
    on rape prosecutions. Ohio's new rape
    law is explained in detail, and comparisons
    are drawn between Ohio's law and similar
    statutes enacted in California and Michigan.
    Major revisions to Ohio's rape law were
    made in the areas of the definition of the
    crime, services to be provided for victims
    of rape, the suppression of records, and
    the admissability of evidence in a rape
    trial. The author criticizes Ohio's new
    rape law on the basis of various
    inconsistencies and weaknesses she finds
    contained in it.

60. Clinch, Nancy Gager and Cathleen Schurr. "Rape."
    WASHINGTONIAN, June 1973, pp. 86-124.

    Clinch and Schurr cite statistics showing
    a steady increase in the incidence of rape
    in the United States. The Metropolitan
    Police Department of the District of
    Columbia's special rape investigation
    unit is described in detail, and possible
    victim reactions to the police are
    mentioned. The authors discuss the
    psychological needs of the rape victim,
    and the legal procedures involved in
    prosecuting a rape case. Women's groups
    organized to provide help and support
    for rape victims are also discussed.

61. "Code R.--for Rape." NEWSWEEK, 80: 75,
    November 13, 1972.

    Many rape victims are receiving aid and
    support from religious personnel. At
    hospitals and clinics connected to the
    University of Chicago, a chaplains'
    counseling service for rape victims has
    been established. The operation of the
    service is discussed, emphasizing the
    improvement shown in treatment for the
    rape victim since the establishment of
    the service.

62. Cohen, Murray L. and Richard J. Boucher.
    "Misunderstandings About Sex Criminals."
    SEXUAL BEHAVIOR, 2: 56-62, March 1972.

    The authors surveyed over one hundred
    people in order to classify their
    conceptions concerning sex criminals.
    Many misconceptions were found among the
    responses of those people surveyed.
    These misconceptions are discussed in
    detail, including misconceptions
    concerning the dangerousness of the
    sex offender, and the prognosis for
    treatability of sexual criminals. The
    authors conclude by providing some
    insight into the psychology of sex
    offenders.

63. Cohen, Murray L. and Theoharis Seghorn.
"Profile of the Rapist." PSYCHIATRIC
SPECTATOR, 6: 17-20, 1971.

In this article, Cohen and Seghorn identify
three basic patterns of rape and discuss
each one in detail. They state that the
rapist who is seduced or provoked into
committing the act by the victim is very
rare, and that each rape has both sexual
and aggressive components. Often the
rape is committed along with another
crime, such as robbery, and the primary
aim of the offender was not to commit
rape. The offender's relationship with
female members of his family is also
discussed.

64. Cohen, Murray L. and others. "The Psychology
of Rapists." SEMINARS IN PSYCHIATRY,
3(3): 307-327, August 1971.

In dealing with the psychological factors
involved in rape, clinical data was
collected at the treatment center, which
had been established by law, in Massachusetts.
Following a critical examination of this
law, the authors proceed to discuss the
rapist and rape in light of this law and
the diagnostic catagories for rapists,
as established by the treatment center.
By presenting a scheme for classifying
rapists according to the motivation
behind the act--a scheme developed by two
other theorists--and by applying this scheme
to specific cases observed at the treatment
center, the authors conclude that the
clinic's classifications are not adequate
in themselves to describe the psychology
behind acts of rape.

65. Cohen, Murray L. and others. "Sociometric
Study of the Sex Offender." JOURNAL OF
ABNORMAL PSYCHOLOGY, 74(2) 249-255, 1969.

Over eight hundred (800) males who had
committed sexually deviant acts were
studied in order to determine the
effectiveness of medicolegal and clinical
classification procedures for the study of
sexually deviant persons. Using a

27

sociometric procedure, the differences
in the efficiency of social skills were
studied. The subjects were also placed
into clinically descriptive catagories
which identified four groups of rapists
and three groups of pedophiles. The
clinical classifications are described
in detail, as is the method which had
been employed for conducting the study.
The authors conclude that the clinical
classification is more valuable for
research of this type than is the
medicolegal grouping. The clinical
classification was also effective in
clarifying sociometric differences in
the study.

66. Cohen, Sharon G. "Constitutional Law--The
    Eighth Amendment's Proscription of Cruel
    and Unusual Punishment Precludes Imposition
    of the Death Sentence for Rape When the
    Victim's Life is Neither Taken Nor
    Endangered--Ralph v. Warden, 438 F.2d 786
    (4th cir. 1970)." THE GEORGE WASHINGTON
    LAW REVIEW, 40(1): 161-172, October 1971.

    This article deals with the constitutionality
    of the imposition of the death penalty in
    a rape case when the victim's life is not
    taken nor threatened. The eighth
    amendment prohibits cruel and unusual
    punishment. In Ralph v. Warden, the case
    which is central to this article, the
    appellate court ruled that the imposition
    of the death penalty in this case would
    constitute cruel and unusual punishment,
    since the victim's life was not endangered.
    Cohen also cites other cases in which
    similar decisions were reached, and
    examines the strengths and weaknesses of
    these cases as well as of the Ralph v.
    Warden case. The Ralph v. Warden case is
    also discussed in light of its possible
    effects on capital punishment in general.
    The author concludes, however, that despite
    its strengths, the Ralph v. Warden decision
    has certain shortcomings, citing the lack
    of established precedents and the vagueness
    of the decision as barriers to proper
    application of the ruling.

67. Cohn, Barbara. "Succumbing to Rape?" THE
    SECOND WAVE: A MAGAZINE OF THE NEW
    FEMINISM, 2(2): 24-27, 1972.

    The issue of consent is discussed from
    a feminist perspective. Cohn emphasizes
    the fact that submission by a rape victim
    does not necessarily imply consent, and
    that many rape victims submit to their
    assailants out of fear for their lives.
    The attitudes of men and some medical
    personnel toward rape and rape victims
    are discussed, with the implication that
    sex role socialization is to blame for
    these attitudes. The victim's fear and
    revulsion at the thought of voluntarily
    engaging in a violent act of retaliation
    against her assailant is also attributed
    to sex role socialization. Cohn concludes
    by stating that a woman who lives in fear
    of rape avoids it by giving up her
    independence and trust in people. An
    independent woman may be forced to
    reconstruct her life in order to follow
    the rules established by men for living
    in a male dominated society without fear
    of repercussions, such as sexual assault.

68. Collins, James W. "Constitutional Law--The
    Texas Equal Rights Amendment--A Rape
    Statute That Only Punishes Men Does Not
    Violate the Texas ERA." TEXAS TECH LAW
    REVIEW, 7: 724-731, Spring 1976.

    In the Texas rape case of Finley v. State,
    527 S.W.2d 553 (Tex. Crim. App. 1975),
    the defendant argued that a statute which
    applied to men and not to women, such as
    the rape statute in Texas law, was
    unconstitutional because it violated the
    Texas Equal Rights Amendment. The court
    held that Finley's claim was without
    substance because a woman who assisted
    in the commission of a rape could also be
    prosecuted and punished under the Texas
    statute, and that the proscriptions of
    Texas's rape laws applied to both men
    and women, even though the definition of
    rape under the statute makes it impossible

for a woman to actually perpetrate the crime. Collins discusses this case, the Texas Equal Rights Amendment, and the impact of the case of <u>Finley v. State</u> on the application of the Equal Rights Amendment in future cases.

69. "Complainant Credibility in Sexual Offense Cases: A Survey of Character Testimony and Psychiatric Experts." THE JOURNAL OF CRIMINAL LAW AND CRIMINOLOGY, 64(1): 67-75, 1973.

In an attempt to guard against false accusations of rape, the courts have developed various safeguards to protect the accused. This article discusses the effectiveness of these safeguards and their impact on the victim, the defendant, and the legal process. Character evidence and psychiatric evidence are discussed and compared. The author also discusses the controversal corroboration requirement, and suggests that an examination of the victim by a psychiatrist and the admission of the psychiatrist's testimony into evidence during the trial, may be a more effective way of assessing the credibility of the complainant.

70. Connell, Noreen and Cassandra Wilson, editors. RAPE: THE FIRST SOURCEBOOK FOR WOMEN. New York: Plume Books, 1974. 283 pages.

This book has been rightly entitled a "sourcebook for women" since it covers practically every aspect of rape. The book is divided into five sections, each section dealing with one aspect of rape. The first section, "Consciousness-Raising: Rape is Carried to its Logical Conclusion," discusses the importance of consciousness-raising groups to an increased understanding of rape. The second section presents a variety of personal statements on rape from the victims themselves. Section three, a section entitled,"Feminist Analysis: The 'Alleged' Victim and the Psycho-Sexual

System," contains six selections, each
one by a different author, which deal with
the psychology of rape, rape and the
process of psychotherapy, the sexual abuse
of children, and rape as it is portrayed
in fiction and films. Rape and the legal
system is the subject of the fourth
section. Three different authors discuss
various aspects of rape and the law:
Edith Barnett discusses the "Legal Aspects
of Rape in New York State," Cassandra
Wilson interviews a feminist lawyer
concerning rape legislation, and Pamela
Lakes Wood explores the role of the
victim in a rape case which is reported
to the police and prosecuted by the court
system. A model rape law, proposed by the
New York University Law School Clinical
Program in Women's Legal Rights, is also
presented in this section. The final
section discusses medical issues involved
in rape cases, the development and
operation of rape crisis centers, methods
of self-defense, the sexual abuse of
children, and political action taken against
rape by women's groups. The appendix also
contains significant information, including:
where to write for pamphlets written on
rape, suggestions for the eradication of
rape, and a three-page bibliography which
lists books, journal articles, and the
titles and addresses of feminist journals
which have published material on rape.

This work also includes a two-page general
bibliography on rape.

71.   "Constitutional Law: Capital Punishment for
        Rape Constitutes Cruel and Unusual
        Punishment When No Life is Taken or
        Endangered." MINNESOTA LAW REVIEW,
        56(1): 95-110, November 1971.

        In the case of Ralph v. Warden, 438F.2d
        786 (4th cir. 1970), the United States
        Supreme Court ruled that the death penalty
        was unconstitutional in rape cases where
        the victim's life was neither taken nor
        endangered. In such cases, the death

31

penalty is disproportionate with the crime and, therefore, constitutes cruel and unusual punishment as prohibited by the eighth amendment to the United States Constitution. This selection comments on various interpretations of "cruel and unusual punishment" and the proportionality of the method of punishment with the crime committed. Standards for determining the cruelty of punishments, the application of these standards, and the abuses associated with them are presented. The case of Ralph v. Warden is discussed in detail, and other cases in which the eighth amendment was an issue are cited.

72.   "The Constitutionality of the Death Penalty for Non-Aggravated Rape." WASHINGTON UNIVERSITY LAW QUARTERLY, 1972(1): 170-178, Winter 1972.

Focusing on the case of Ralph v. Warden, 438F.2d 786 (4th cir. 1970), the issue of the constitutionality of the death penalty for rape is explored. The eighth amendment to the U.S. Constitution prohibits cruel and unusual punishment. It is argued that, in the case of Ralph v. Warden, the death penalty for non-aggravated rape was disproportionate to the severity of the crime committed and, therefore, constituted cruel and usual punishment as prohibited by the eighth amendment. In exploring this issue, other cases of rape in which the death penalty had been an issue are discussed. The article concludes by stating that in order for a court to determine whether a punishment is cruel and unusual, standards must be established for making the determination. Instead of establishing necessary standards, many courts have relied on public sentiment and societal attitudes toward the crime as criteria for making a determination as to the proportionality of punishments.

73. Copeland, Lorraine. "The Queen's Bench
        Foundation's Project Rape Response."
        VICTIMOLOGY: AN INTERNATIONAL JOURNAL,
        1(2): 331-337, Summer 1976.

        The Queen's Bench Foundation conducted a
        year-long rape victimization study in
        San Francisco, California. For the first
        six months of the project, the foundation
        studied the social and psychological
        impact of rape, the needs of the rape
        victim, procedures of medical and criminal
        justice personnel for handling rape cases,
        services within the community which are
        available to victims, and reasons for the
        underreporting of rapes. The remaining
        six months of the project were devoted
        to improving the services available to
        victims and the responses of medical and
        law enforcement personnel. Copeland
        discusses the problems associated with
        rape in the San Francisco area, the
        goals and objectives of the project, and
        the findings of the study.

74. Cormier, Bruno M. and Siebert P. Simons.
        "The Problem of the Dangerous Sexual
        Offender." CANADIAN PSYCHIATRIC
        ASSOCIATION JOURNAL, 14(4): 329-335,
        August 1969.

        Cormier and Simons studied sex offenders
        who are prone to violent behavior, such as
        murder or repeated forcible rape. Such
        crimes elicit strong responses from the
        public, including a desire for retribution.
        The authors attempt to learn if the
        dangerous sexual offender can be isolated
        through the use of clinical methods. A
        significant factor in identifying the
        degree of dangerousness of a sexual
        offender is the presence of a progressive
        record. The offender's choice of victim
        and the characteristics of the offense
        are discussed as reflections of the
        offender's psychopathology. The authors
        conclude that although the percentage of
        dangerous sexual offenders is relatively
        small, they constitute a major problem

for society. These offenders have a high
recidivism rate and seldom receive appropriate
treatment. Early identification of the truly
dangerous sexual offender is suggested as a
method of preventing violent sexual crimes.

75. "Corroborating Charges of Rape." COLUMBIA
     LAW REVIEW, 67: 1137-1148, 1967.

     This note examines the controversal
     corroboration requirement for rape cases
     in New York State. Justifications for
     the existence of a corroboration
     requirement, acceptable methods for
     corroborating a charge of rape, and the
     scope of New York State's requirement
     are discussed in detail.

76. "The Corroboration Rule and Crimes Accompanying
     a Rape." UNIVERSITY OF PENNSYLVANIA LAW
     REVIEW, 118(3): 458-472, January 1970.

     Many states require stringent corroborating
     evidence, in addition to the victim's
     testimony, in order to prove that a rape
     had been committed. In cases where another
     crime, such as robbery, had been committed
     during the course of the rape, does the
     corroboration requirement apply to these
     crimes as it does to the accompanying
     crime of rape? This question was an
     important issue in the New York case of
     People v. Moore, 23 N.Y .2d 565, N.E.
     .2d 710, 297 N.Y.S.2d 944, cert. denied,
     394, U.S. 1006 (1969). Moore was
     convicted of robbery, grand larceny, and
     attempted rape by a New York Court. On
     appeal, the intermediate appellate court
     ruled that the larceny and robbery
     convictions stand, but that the attempted
     rape conviction by reversed, and Moore
     be retried for that offense. The defendant
     then appealed to the New York State Court
     of Appeals on the grounds that the larceny
     and robbery convictions should not be
     sustained upon the same uncorroborated
     evidence admitted to prove rape, since no
     specific intent to commit robbery or
     larceny had been proven. The court affirmed
     the robbery and larceny convictions,

reasoning that the crimes were not
"committed in aid of effecting rape,"
nor were they directly related to the
rape itself. This article discusses the
corroboration rule and the problems which
led to its adoption in New York State.
The extension and implementation of the
rule are also explored.

77. "Criminal Law--Evidence--Corroboration Held
Necessary to Prove Sexual Abuse in the
Third Degree Where the Underlying Act is
Rape." NEW YORK UNIVERSITY LAW REVIEW,
44(5): 1025-1033, November 1969.

This selection is based on a New York case,
People v. Doyle, 31 App. Div. 2d490, 300
N.Y.S.2d 719 (2d Dep't 1969), in which the
court held that there must be corroborating
evidence in order to prove sexual abuse in
the third degree if it is shown that the
act of rape was committed. The court
also noted that there must be corroborating
evidence in any case of assault in which
a rape had been committed. The author
suggests that a more exact definition of
what constitutes sufficient corroboration
in rape cases is necessary, and that if
sexual abuse in the third degree is to
be exempt from the corroboration requirement,
the exemption should apply to all crimes
so charged, even if the underlying act
committed is rape.

78. "Criminal Law--Prosection for Assault With
Intent to Rape Is Permissable Even After
a Prior Acquittal for Rape and a Present
Intent to Rape in the Future Completes
the Offense." TEXAS LAW REVIEW, 51:
360-368, January 1973.

The issue central to this selection is
whether a defendant who had been acquitted
for the offense of rape can be found
guilty of assault with intent to rape, in
the same case. If so, does the verdict
constitute harassment? These questions
are discussed by referring to the case of
Douthit v. State, 482 S.W.2d 155 (Tex.
Crim. App. 1971), and other cases which

had also dealt with this issue, or with
related issues. The problem of future
intent is discussed, and the question
harassment in this case is explored.

79.   "Criminal Law--Rape--Cautionary Instruction in
      Sex Offense Trial Relating Prosecutrix's
      Credibility to the Nature of the Crime
      Charged Is No Longer Mandatory;
      Discretionary Use Is Disapproved."
      FORDHAM URBAN LAW JOURNAL, 4: 419-430,
      Winter 1976.

      This note comments on the California case,
      People v. Rincon-Pindea, 14 Cal. 3d 864,
      538 P.2d 247, 123 Cal. Rptr. 119 (1975).
      The defendant appealed his rape conviction,
      alleging that the judge had been in error
      by not giving the mandatory cautionary
      instruction which stated that the crime
      of rape is an easy one to charge, but a
      difficult one to prove, and the victim's
      testimony must be examined with caution.
      The California Supreme Court upheld the
      conviction, stating that the cautionary
      instruction should have been given, but
      that the judge's error was not prejudicial.
      The court also prohibited the mandatory
      application of the instruction in the
      future, and urged the rewording of it
      for possible discretionary use, although
      the court openly disapproved the
      discretionary use of the instruction.
      The origin and application of the cautionary
      instruction are discussed, and the
      importance of using a cautionary instruction
      only in conjuction with specific evidence
      presented in a particular case is suggested.

80.   Cross, Rupert. "Centenary Reflections on
      Prince's Case." THE LAW QUARTERLY
      REVIEW, 91: 540-553, October 1975.

      Central to this article is the author's
      belief that people who commit crimes
      should be judged on the facts as they
      had perceived them at the time of the
      offense. In the case of R. v. Prince
      (1875) L.R. 2 C.C.R. 154, the defendant

had abducted a thirteen year old girl,
believing that she was eighteen. When
convicted in a court of law for abduction,
Prince was sentenced to three months
imprisonment with hard labor. Cross
discusses the Prince case and concludes
that the principle of mistaken age, as
illustrated by this case, is definitely
applicable in cases of statutory rape
and should be considered as a defense
in statutory rape cases.

81. "Cruel and Unusual Punishment--Constitutionality
of the Death Penalty For Rape Where the
Victim's Life is Neither Taken Nor Endangered
--Ralph v. Warden, 438 F.2d 786 (4th cir.
1970)." RICHMOND LAW REVIEW, 5: 392-400,
Spring 1971.

Although many courts have attempted to
define the meaning of "cruel and unusual"
as contained in the eighth amendment's
proscription against the imposition of
cruel and unusual punishment, no universal
definition has been formulated to date.
Arguements both for and against the death
penalty are provided, and the death penalty
as a punishment for rape is discussed.
The court in Ralph v. Warden held that the
death penalty in a rape case where the
victim's life is neither taken nor
endangered is unconstitutional according
to the eighth amendment's proscription in
the United States Constitution. The
death penalty in this case was viewed as
being disproportionate to the culpability
of the defendant and would, therefore,
constitute cruel and unusual punishment.

82. Crum, Roger S. "Counseling Rape Victims."
THE JOURNAL OF PASTORAL CARE, 28(2):
112-121, June 1974.

Recognizing the need for a treatment
program to aid rape victims in coping
with the psychological trauma experienced
by victims as a result of a sexual
assault, a three-phase treatment procedure

was initiated by the staff of a Chicago,
Illinois hospital. The first phase
involved the establishment of a policy
which gave medical priority to rape
cases when immediate, emergency care
was necessary. The two subsequent
phases of the program provided for a
chaplain to be called in for counseling
in rape cases, and for the integration
of the Department of Gynecology of
the hospital into the treatment
procedure. The psychological needs
of the rape victim and the corresponding
responsibilities of the chaplain in
counseling victims are also discussed.
Crum cites the success of the program,
and its effect on changing the attitudes
of many police and hospital personnel
toward rape and rape victims.

83. Cryer, Linda. "Rape Examination: A Prescription
for Medico-Legal Procedures." VICTIMOLOGY:
AN INTERNATIONAL JOURNAL, 1(2): 337-341,
Summer 1976.

In order to provide efficient treatment
for the rape victim, the city of Houston,
Texas developed a standardized procedure
for the collection, routing, and analysis
of medical evidence. This procedure,
which involves the use of a special
evidence packet, is described in detail.
The packet contains items necessary for
a complete evidence collection and
analysis procedure: instructions for the
collection, routing, and analysis of
the evidence, an examination form, and
specimen containers. The role of the
physician in the collection and
analysis process is clearly stated, and
strict guidelines are drawn which
differentiate this role from the role
of the legal and criminal justice
personnel in the processing of a rape
complaint.

84. Csida, June Bundy and Joseph Csida. RAPE:
    HOW TO AVOID IT, AND WHAT TO DO ABOUT
    IT IF YOU CAN'T. Chatsworth, California:
    Books for Better Living, 1974. 238 pages.

    The authors present an extensive work
    on the problem of rape. To illustrate
    the extent of the problem, some recent
    rape cases are discussed. The impact of
    the crime upon the victim, the psychology
    of the rapist, legal and medical
    treatment of rape complaints, the
    emergence of rape crisis centers, and
    methods of rape prevention are among the
    topics explored in this book. The
    organization and operation of the New
    York City Police Department's Rape
    Investigation and Analysis section, a
    checklist for victims which had been
    developed by the New York City Police
    Department, and excerpts from Senator
    Mathias's presentation of bill number
    S.2422 (the Rape Prevention and Control
    Act) to the United States Senate are also
    included.

85. Curtis, Lynn A. "Present and Future Measures
    of Victimization in Forcible Rape."
    in: Walker, Marcia J. and Stanley L.
    Brodsky, editors, SEXUAL ASSAULT.
    Lexington, Massachusetts: Lexington
    Books, 1976, pp. 61-68.

    Curtis examines methods used for
    measuring rape victimization. The
    methods discussed include material in
    police records, and reports of the Law
    Enforcement Assistance Administration-
    Census National Crime Panel. The
    author also discusses some problems
    involved in the collection of accurate
    victimization statistics and the need for
    innovations in methods for gathering
    statistics. Some suggestions for
    improving methods of gathering
    victimization information are presented.

86. Curtis, Lynn A. "Rape, Race, and Culture:
        Some Speculations in Search of a Theory."
        in: Walker, Marcia J. and Stanley L.
        Brodsky, editors, SEXUAL ASSAULT.
        Lexington, Massachusetts: Lexington Books,
        1976, pp. 117-134.

        Curtis states that data from studies and
        reports show that a larger portion of
        rapes are committed by non-whites than
        by whites, although the rates appear to
        be disproportionate with the proportion
        of non-whites to whites in the entire
        population. The focus of this article
        is on the black offender, examining
        the value space of blacks, the "black
        poverty subculture," the "violent
        counterculture," and determinism in
        respect to race and socioecomonic
        constraints. Inter-racial and intra-
        racial rapes are also discussed. Curtis
        suggests that culture falls between the
        outcomes of sexual assault and the
        inequalities of the social structure,
        and that a "refined conceptualization"
        integrating many political, social,
        and psychological variables is needed
        in order to understand rape.

87. Davis, Angela. "Joanne Little: The Dialectics
        of Rape." MS. MAGAZINE, 3(12): 74-77,
        and 106-108, June 1975.

        Joanne Little, a twenty year-old black
        woman who had been serving a prison
        term of seven to ten years for larceny,
        breaking and entering, and receiving
        stolen property in a North Carolina
        jail, was charged with first degree
        murder in the death of her white, male
        jailer. Little claimed to have stabbed
        the jailer with an ice pick in order to
        defend herself against him during a
        sexual assault. An autopsy performed on
        the jailer indicated that there was
        evidence of recent sexual activity at the
        time of his death, and the condition of
        Little's jail cell indicated that there
        had been a struggle. Davis feels that
        the Little case exemplifies the "myths

of white superiority and male supremacy,"
To illustrate this point, the rape of
black women by white men is discussed
from an historical perspective which
emphasizes the relative absence of
convictions for rape where the accused
is white and the victim is black.
Rape is viewed as a function of the
social, political, and legal systems
in this country, which encourage rape
by promulgating the myth of male
supremacy. This article concludes
with a plea for just legal treatment
in the case of Joanne Little, and a
call for unity among the victims and
opponents of sexism and racism.

88. DeFrancis, Vincent. "Protecting the Child
    Victim of Sex Crimes Committed By Adults."
    FEDERAL PROBATION, 35(3): 15-20,
    September 1971.

    Children who are victims of sex crimes are
    frequently neglected by their families and
    by the community. The victim's physical
    condition and emotional trauma may
    require special treatment, which is not
    always provided. The author explores
    the extent and nature of the sexual
    abuse of children by adults, and discusses
    some of the special services that the
    child victim may require. Reasons why
    people report the sexual abuse of a
    child, problems in the family which may
    lead to the neglect and sexual abuse
    of children, characteristics of child
    victims, and the degree of participation
    or non-participation by the victim in
    the act are also discussed. DeFrancis
    raises questions concerning the lack of
    protective services for children, and
    suggests early intervention into unstable
    families as a protective measure against
    possible child neglect and abuse.

89. Del Drago, Maria. "The Pride of Inez
        Garcia." MS. MAGAZINE, 3(11):
        49, May 1975.

    The author of this selection had been
    a victim of forcible rape, but had felt
    too humiliated to report the crime to the
    authorities. In this article, Del Drago
    parallels her social background and her
    feelings about sexuality and rape with
    those of Inez Garcia. Garcia's trial
    is seen by the author as sexist and
    racist, and justice for Garcia is
    viewed as no justice at all.

90. Derr, Allen R. "Criminal Justice: A Crime
        Against Women?" TRIAL MAGAZINE,
        pp. 24-26, Novemver-December 1973.

    Discrimination in the Criminal Justice
    System on the basis of sex is discussed
    in this article. A brief portion of
    this selection is devoted specifically
    to rape, both forcible and statutory.
    Derr advocates the elimination of
    statutory rape laws and recommends
    that all sexual assaults be treated
    similarly, regardless of the age or
    sex of the victims. Penalties
    established according to the severity
    of the offense committed are also
    urged.

91. District of Columbia Task Force On Rape.
        "Report." in: Schultz, LeRoy, editor,
        RAPE VICTIMOLOGY. Springfield,
        Illinois: Charles C. Thomas, 1975,
        pp. 339-373.

    The full text of the District of
    Columbia Citizen's Task Force on
    Rape is provided, including recommendations
    for reform in present methods or laws
    relevant to rape. The primary targets for
    reform include the laws, the court system,
    police behavior, police procedure, and
    hospital procedure for treating rape
    cases. The report emphasizes the need
    for uniformity in matters concerning

rape, in order to eliminate the
differential treatment given to the
crime by society in general, medical
and social service agencies, and the
criminal justice system.

92. Dodson, Mildred B. "People v. Rincon-Pineda:
Rape Trials Depart the Seventeenth
Century--Farewell to Lord Hale."
TULSA LAW JOURNAL, 11: 279-290, 1975.

In seventeenth century Britain, Lord
Chief Justice Matthew Hale, in his
discussion of felony rape, stated that
rape is an easy accusation to make,
but a difficult one to prove, and
testimony given by the victim during
the trial should be considered by the
jury cautiously and carefully.
Although Hale was making reference to
uncorroborated testimony made by child
witnesses, the statement was eventually
transformed into a cautionary instruction
which was made mandatory in all rape
trials, regardless of the age of the
victim. In the case of People v. Rincon-
Pineda, 14 Cal. 3d 864, 538 P.2d 247,
123 Cal Rptr. 119 (1975), the California
Supreme Court ruled that the cautionary
instruction should not be a mandatory
address to the jury in a rape trial.
This selection discusses the case of
People v. Rincon-Pineda and its effect
on appellate review. The decision in
this case is seen as an attempt by the
court to elevate the status of the
victim in a rape trial, which may, in
turn, provide an incentive for other
victims to prosecute their assailants.

93. Douglas, Carol Ann. "Rape in Literature."
THE SECOND WAVE: A MAGAZINE OF THE NEW
FEMINISM, 2(2): 29-30, 1972.

The image of rape as presented in
literature by male novelists reflects
the attitudes toward rape in a male
dominated society. Douglas describes
incidents of rape in some popular

novels, stating that although the
authors' approaches to the subject of
rape are quite different, the
underlying assumption of rape as an
exciting, pleasant, and welcomed
experience for the victim is usually
the same.

94. Dworkin, Roger B. "The Resistance Standard in
Rape Legislation." STANFORD LAW REVIEW,
18: 680-689, 1966.

The author recognizes the need for some
kind of unifying principle in rape
statutes in order to aid in the sentencing
of offenders. The absence of adequate
standards for sentencing is discussed.
The elimination of the consent standard
in its present form is encouraged,
since its primary purposes seem to be
to be to preserve women's roles in
society, and to bolster "masculine pride."
The author advocates the adoption of
the resistance standard in place of the
consent standard. The resistance
standard is based not on the question
of the consent of the victim, but on
her actual conduct in the rape
situation. By focusing on the conduct
of the victim, an objective standard for
determining whether a rape had actually
occurred may be formulated. Dworkin
examines the resistance standard in
detail, discussing resistance and
forcible rape, the element of resistance
in catagorizing sex offenses, and elements of
resistance in determining various degrees of
rape. A detailed model rape statute is
suggested, and the adoption of a similar
statute is advocated as a method for
defining rape and related offenses,
and distinguishing between them for the
purpose of sentencing offenders.

95. Eckert, William G. "Forensic Aspects of
    Sex Crimes and Problems." INFORM,
    3: 3-7, 1971.

    Specific problems facing forensic
    personnel when dealing with the
    investigations of sex crimes are
    identified and explained. A procedure
    for a medico-legal investigation of
    sexual offenses is outlined in chart
    form. Eckert also discusses sex crimes
    which result in the death of the victim
    by murder or by other forms of unnatural
    death, such as accidential electrocution.

96. Edelson, Carol. "Women and the Law: Rape."
    OFF OUR BACKS, 9(4): 24, March 1974.

    The problems facing a woman lawyer in
    defending a rapist are discussed. A
    woman legal aid attorney states that
    although she, as a feminist, does not feel
    comfortable defending a rapist, a male
    defense attorney may give the rape victim
    a difficult time when questioning her
    in court. It is also emphasized that
    a victim may be more comfortable and
    less traumatized by the presence of a
    woman defense attorney, than by a
    man in the same position. The
    reluctance of a woman to report a rape
    is also discussed, and the need for
    support from the victim's family and
    friends is emphasized. Knowledge of
    the presence of women police personnel
    may also encourage the victim of a
    rape to report the crime.

97. Eisenberg, Robert L. "Abolishing Cautionary
    Instructions in Sex Offense Cases:
    People v. Rincon-Pineda." CRIMINAL
    LAW BULLETIN, 12(1): 58-72, January-
    February 1976.

    For over three-hundred years, it was
    mandatory for the court to instruct
    the jury in a rape trial to be cautious
    in examining evidence given by the
    complainant because the crime of rape

is an easy crime to charge, but a
difficult one to defend against. In
the case of People v. Rincon-Pineda,
14 Cal. 3d 864, 538 P.2d 247, 123 Cal.
Rptr. 119 (1975), the Supreme Court
of California ruled that this instruction
cease to be mandatory. The Court also
prohibited the use of this particular
cautionary instruction as presently
worded. The author of this selection
presents the facts and the decision in
People v. Rincon-Pineda, and discusses the
law and the use of the cautionary
instruction prior to the decision in the
case of People v. Rincon-Pineda. The
issue of the denial of due process in
regard to the abolition of the mandatory
cautionary instruction is void in light
of the Chief Justice's instructions
specifying that an instruction be given
concerning the credibility of the witnesses
in the case. Eisenberg comments on the
balancing of the rights of the defendant
and the victim involved in Rincon-Pineda
and discusses its significance for the
treatment of victims of rape by the
legal system.

98.   Eisenbud, Frederick. "Limitations on the
      Right to Introduce Evidence Pertaining
      to the Prior Sexual History of the
      Complaining Witness in Cases of Forcible
      Rape: Reflection of Reality or Denial of
      Due Process?" HOFSTRA LAW REVIEW, 3:
      403-426, Spring 1975.

      The issue of consent in a rape trial is
      discussed in detail. Background information
      concerning the issue of consent and the
      limits of the admissibility of evidence
      to prove consent is provided. The
      admissibility of a victim's prior
      sexual history into evidence in a rape
      trial is a controversial issue.
      Eisenbud discussed the relevancy of such
      evidence and the primary reasons why
      this evidence may be excluded from
      admissibility during the trial.
      Controversy over this issue centers
      around the defendant's constitutional

right to confront and cross-examine
witnesses called by the state to
testify against him during the trial.
The author concludes that it is the
defendant's constitutional right to
confront witnesses called to give
evidence against him during the trial,
but until a general determination can
be made that a woman's prior sexual
history reflects the probability that she
will consent to intercourse on a certain
occasion, the court, at its discretion,
is unable to rule all such evidence as
irrelevant and, therefore, inadmissable.

99. Enos, W.F., J.C. Beyer, and G.T. Mann.
The Medical Examination of Cases of
Rape." JOURNAL OF FORENSIC SCIENCES,
17(1): 50-56, 1972.

Following a brief discussion of the
adequacy of medical examinations of alleged
rape victims, the authors provide a
detailed description of the procedure
followed by physicians in the northern
area of Virginia. The taking of a
history, the observation of the victim's
emotional state immediately following
the alleged assault, a physical
examination, and the collection of specimens
for laboratory analysis are among the
procedures discussed.

100. "Evidence--Admissibility--In a Trial for Rape,
Prosecutrix May Not Be Cross-Examined As
To Specific Acts of Prior Sexual Conduct
With Men Other Than Defendant, Whether
the Prupose of Such Cross-Examination Is
to Establish Her Consent as an Affirmative
Defense or to Impeach Her Credibility As
a Witness." GEORGIA LAW REVIEW, 8: 973-
983, Summer 1974.

In Lynn v. State,231 Ga. 559, 203 S.E.2d
221 (1974), the Supreme Court of Georgia
held that victim's prior sexual conduct
with men other than the defendant is not
admissable as evidence in a rape case.
This selection discusses the case of

Lynn v. State and refers to other cases relevant to the Lynn case. The arguement is made that testimony concerning a victim's past sexual history is relevant to the issue of consent in a rape trial and should, therefore, be admitted into evidence. It is the opinon of the author that in ruling on the case of Lynn v. State, important issues were ignored, and the court based its decision on precedents which had never been properly decided.

101. Evrard, John R. "Rape: The Medical, Social, and Legal Implications." AMERICAN JOURNAL OF OBSTETRICS AND GYNECOLOGY, 111: 197-199, September 15, 1971.

The author focuses on the medical examination of a rape victim. Procedures followed by a physician in examining a sexual assault victim, and the collection of medical evidence for the court, are explained in detail. Legal definitions of rape, and the protection of a patient's legal rights in a rape case, are also discussed. In addition to the importance of careful attention to details when taking a patient's medical history and conducting the medical examination, Evrard emphasizes the need for sympathetic counseling of the rape victim.

102. "The Facts on Rape." HUMAN BEHAVIOR, 2(6): 49-50, June 1973.

As the title implies, this selection deals very generally with the problem of rape. Rape is discussed as a seasonable crime, with most rapes occurring from the months of May to October. The amount of violence employed by the assailant, victim and offender characteristics, and the geographical locations where the majority of rapes occur are also discussed. Most of the information in this selection was gathered by Norman S. Goldner, who believes that the

literature available on the subject
of rape is insufficient, and that if
progress is to be made in reducing the
number of rapes in this country, a better
understanding of the crime is necessary.

103. Feegel, John R. "Synopsis of Rape for the
Florida Examiner." JOURNAL OF THE
FLORIDA MEDICAL ASSOCIATION, 56: 729-
730, September 1969.

Feegel summarizes the Florida statutes
pertaining to sex offenses and discusses
the procedures involved in examining the
victim of sexual assault, including the
child victim. The examination of
statutory rape cases is also discussed,
focusing on elements unique to these
cases. The role of the medical
examiner, as established by the Florida
Legislature, is explained.

104. Findlay, Barbara. "The Cultural Context of
Rape." WOMEN LAWYERS JOURNAL, 60:
199-207, Fall 1974.

Rape is discussed as a form of social
interaction in which social and economic
organizations contribute to its
development and growth. The author
compares the economic and social systems
of two very differently structured
societies, emphasizing the notions of
male and female roles, and sexuality,
within each society. Following this
comparison, some general characteristics
of rapists are presented, focusing on
the fact that the typical rapist is not
always a "sex maniac," but someone
considered to be "normal" and known to
the victim. Also, the myth that the
majority of women who cry rape are
leveling false accusations, and that
most convicted rapists are actually
innocent is not supported in this article.
Findlay concludes that by educating the
public about the realities of rape,
eradicating the myths surrounding rape,
and not unjustly questioning the credibility

of a legitimate rape victim, more
victims will be encouraged to report
the crimes, and more rapists will be
brought to trial and convicted for
their offenses.

105. Fisher, Gary and E. Rivlin. "Psychological
Needs of Rapists." BRITISH JOURNAL OF
CRIMINOLOGY, 11: 182-185, 1971.

The psychological needs of rapists are
examined using the Edwards Personal
Preference Schedule (EPPS). This
test studies the needs of criminal
sexual offenders and compares them with
the needs of other male offenders, and
those of non-criminal males. The authors
found the rapists studied to have need
structures different from those of
other male offenders and those of the
non-criminal males examined. They
conclude that rapists tend to be less
independent, less dominant, less
self-assured, less aggressive, more
critical of themselves, and have a
higher heterosexual drive than do other
male offenders or non-criminal adult
males.

106. Flammang, C.J. "Interviewing Child Victims
of Sex Offenders." in: Schultz, LeRoy G.,
editor, RAPE VICTIMOLOGY. Springfield,
Illinois: Charles C. Thomas, 1975,
pp. 245-256.

There are many forms of sexual behavior
encountered by children in which the
child may or may not be a willing
participant. When a sex offense directed
toward a child is reported to law
enforcement personnel, the police must
question the victim concerning various
aspects of the offense. Flammang
discusses problems encountered by police
in questioning child victims. Police
procedure for interviewing a child
victim is cited, emphasizing the
importance of the child's testimony as a
witness for the state in the event that

the offender is brought to trial and prosecuted for the offense. Examples of questions used in the police interview of the child victim of a rape or other sex offense are also provided.

107. Fox, Sandra Sutherland and Donald J. Scherl. "Crisis Intervention With Victims of Rape." SOCIAL WORK, 43(1): 37-42, January 1972.

According to Fox and Scherl, the rape victim goes through three sequential stages of emotional reaction to the assault. A detailed explanation of each stage, including the medical treatment and contact with legal, social, and psychiatric services that may occur during the stage under discussion, are presented. The authors conclude by exploring the possibility that their plan for crisis intervention with victims of rape may have implications for prevention of the crime.

108. Foxe, Arthur N. "Rape, Rats, and Reflection. Crime: The Broad View." CORRECTIVE PSYCHIATRY AND JOURNAL OF SOCIAL THERAPY, 14(4): 213-223, Winter 1968.

The original meaning of the word rape was not sexual: Rape referred to the abduction of a person, either male or female. With the aid of references from myths and Roman history, Foxe describes the development of the definition of rape into what it is today. The New York State Penal Law pertaining to rape is defined and briefly discussed. Much of this article, however, deals with political and legal issues only distantly related to the crime of rape itself.

109. Frank, Arthur and Stuart Frank. "Medical
     Aspects of Rape." MADEMOISELLE, 82:
     46 and 68, February 1976.

     Primary areas of concern for the
     physician in dealing with rape victims
     are identified as pregnancy, venereal
     disease, physical injuries, and emotional
     problems. The authors discuss these
     problems in light of the victim's
     immediate needs and necessary follow-up
     treatment. Emphasis is placed on the
     victim's emotional condition immediately
     following the assault. Suggestions are
     made for treatment ained at reducing
     the victim's psychological trauma, which
     is a major area of concern for the
     attending physician.

110. Gaensbauer, Theodore J. "Castration in
     Treatment of Sex Offenders." ROCKY
     MOUNTAIN MEDICAL JOURNAL, 70: 23-28,
     April 1973.

     Gaensbauer discusses the literature
     pertaining to castration as a treatment
     for sexual deviancy, in an effort to
     discover if castration has a therapeutic
     value in treating the sex offender.
     Reference is made to research showing that
     psychological factors are responsible for
     sexual deviations, rather than physiological
     ones, as is frequently assumed. Thus,
     a physiological rather than a psychological
     method of treatment would not be an
     effective method for treating the sex
     offender. Gaensbauer mentions the
     irreversibility of castration, with its
     possible disabling physiological and
     psychological side effects, and suggests,
     as a treatment method, the use of drugs
     which produce the same effects as
     castration, but without the complications,
     if a physiological method of treatment
     is desired.

111. Gager, Nancy and Cathleen Schurr. SEXUAL
     ASSAULT: CONFRONTING RAPE IN AMERICA.
     New York: Grosset and Dunlop, 1976.
     336 pages.

     Rape is, perhaps, the most ambiguous
     crime in America. Victims of sexual
     assault are frequently misunderstood,
     and their needs are often overlooked.
     Gager and Schurr examine the problem of
     rape with this basic framework, exploring
     controversal areas such as societal
     reaction to the crime and to the victim,
     psychological effects of the crime for
     the victim, rape in marriage, inadequacies
     in institutions dealing with rape victims,
     and the high recidivism rate among
     convicted rapists. Areas which have been
     virtually unexplored by writers on the
     subject of rape are throughly discussed
     in this book. Actual accounts of gang
     rape, rapes of children, and the rape
     of elderly women are also related.
     The book ends with a rather optimistic
     look toward the future, as far as an
     increased understanding of rape is
     concerned. The authors feel that women
     are determined to do something about
     preventing rape. Some recent advances
     concerning legal reform are cited as
     steps in this direction, but Gager and
     Schurr feel that societal and cultural
     attitudes must be changed before reforms
     can be completely effective.

     This work also contains a twenty-page
     general bibliography of materials
     written on the subject of rape.

112. Gagnon, John H. "Female Child Victims of
     Sex Offenses." SOCIAL PROBLEMS,
     13: 176-192, 1965.

     Following a discussion of the criminal-
     victim relationship in general, and the
     child victim in particular, the author
     presents the findings of his own study
     of the reports of adults concerning their
     victimization as children. The sample
     chosen for study was divided into four
     groups, based on the types of victim

participation which had occurred during the incident. Gagnon discusses the extent of reporting by the victim to the victim's parents and/or to the police, the sexual techniques employed during the offense, the age of the victim, the relationship between the victim and the offender, and the victim's responses immediately following the assault. The effect of the assault upon the victim's sexual adjustment in adult life is also discussed. This article concludes by stating that sexual assaults on children are definitely underreported due to the reluctance of parents to report the offenses to the police.

113. Galton, Eric R. "Police Processing of Rape Complaints: A Case Study." AMERICAN JOURNAL OF CRIMINAL LAW, 4(1): 15-30, Winter 1975-1976.

The procedures involved in the processing of rape complaints by the police is discussed in detail. Included in this discussion is the disposition of rape complaints, the attitudes of investigators concerning rape complaints, and the importance of various types of evidence to the initial investigation. Possible changes to the existing procedures used by police in investigating rape cases are suggested. Galton concludes with statements concerning the importance of strong ties between the police and social service agencies in providing necessary support to the rape victim.

114. Garrett, Thomas B. and Richard Wright. "Wives of Rapists and Incest Offenders." JOURNAL OF SEX RESEARCH, 11(2): 149-157, May 1975.

Garrett and Wright interviewed the wives of convicted sex offenders. The women, all volunteers, were part of a therapy program which had been developed

by a California hospital for patients
convicted of sex crimes, and whose
family situation was believed to have
been instrumental in the offender
committing the crime. The authors
discovered that, in general, the wives
had received more education than had
their husbands, and that their husbands'
crimes served to make the wives morally
and socially stronger than before, even
to the point of reinforcing any
dominant position that they may have
held in their marriages. All of the
women interviewed felt that their
husbands' behaviors had not adversely
affected their marriages.

115. Geis, Gilbert. "Group Sexual Assaults."
MEDICAL ASPECTS OF HUMAN SEXUALITY,
5(5): 101-112, May 1971.

The participants in an act of group
rape act in accordance with established
principles of group behavior. The
group has a leader who plans the assault
and is the first participant to have
intercourse with the victim. In
participating in a group rape, the
assailants feel obligated to play a
certain role in accordance with the
expectations of the other members of
the group. Thus, his actions in
completing the rape are in response to the
other members of the group as well as to
the victim. Geis presents case studies
to illustrate the principles applicable
in group sexual assault. Regarding the
extent of group sexual assaults in the
United States, accurate statistics on
group rapes are not known, however,
statistics from Menachem Amir's study
of rape in Philadelphia, Pennsylvania
indicate that seventy-one percent (71%)
of all reported rapes in that city were
group rapes. The psychology of group
sexual assault is discussed by Geis,
who supplements his own findings with
information from Amir's study.

116. Giles, Linda E. "The Admissibility of a Rape-
        Complainant's Previous Sexual Conduct:
        The Need for Legislative Reform."
        NEW ENGLAND LAW REVIEW, 11: 497-507,
        Spring 1976.

        The need for legislative reform in the
        rule concerning the admissibility of a
        victim's prior sexual history into
        evidence at a rape trial is discussed,
        using the Criminal Code of Massachusetts
        as an example. The Massachusetts Senate
        Bill Number 1961 seeks to prohibit the
        admissibility of a woman's prior sexual
        conduct or reputation into evidence as
        a means of impeaching the victim's
        credibility. This bill and its
        implications are discussed, including
        pertainent legal and political
        considerations. Giles concludes by
        emphasizing the need for a re-evaluation
        of attitudes toward rape and rape victims,
        and reform of present rules of evidence
        regarding a victim's prior sexual history.

117. Gillelson, N. "Avoiding Rape: Whose Advice
        Should You Take?" McCALLS, 103(8):
        66, May 1976.

        The topic of rape prevention is a
        controversial one, and there are many
        opinons as to the best preventative
        measures available to a potential
        rape victim. There are obvious,
        common-sense type precautions, such as
        walking on well-lighted streets and
        avoiding empty subway cars. In addition,
        many self-proclaimed authorities on rape
        and rape prevention have blossomed
        recently. Gillelson quotes a prominent
        social scientist, Dr. Robert Lamb of
        Columbia University, who suggests that
        a "rape industry" has developed in this
        country, in which various people are
        "exploiting and profiting from the
        terror of women" by offering contradictory,
        and often dangerous, advice for preventing
        rape. Lamb feels that because each rape

situation is different, there are no
definite rules for guarenteed success in
the area of rape prevention, and that
each woman must depend on her own
instincts for determining the best method
to employ in her particular situation.

118. Gless, Alan G. "Nebraska's Corroboration Rule."
NEBRASKA LAW REVIEW, 54(1): 93-110, 1975.

The author supports the Nebraska Supreme
Court's decision to retain the corroboration
rule in rape cases in that state. He feels
that this rule imposes stricter burdens
of proof on the state, thus resolving
conflicts concerning the credibility of
the complainant. The corroboration
rule is explained and analyzed, and the
1973 Nebraska case of State v. Fisher,
190 Neb. 742, 212 N.W.2d 568 (1973),
is used to illustrate the need for the
corroboration rule. Gless concludes by
stating that the Nebraska Sepreme Court
is protecting "individual liberty by
preventing convictions based on unreliable
evidence" by retaining the corroboration
rule.

119. Goldfarb, Ronald. "Rape and Law Reform."
WASHINGTON POST, p. A-24, August 2, 1973.

The City Council's Public Safety Committee's
Task Force on Rape (Washington, D.C.)
reports that, "Rape is the fastest growing
crime of violence in the District of
Columbia," and yet the most under-reported.
These facts may be attributed to the
ineffectiveness of the Criminal Justice
System in deterring potential rapists, the
low conviction rate for the crime, the
mishandling of rape complaints by the police,
the hospitals, district attorneys, and the
courts. Goldfarb discusses the findings
of the task force on rape, emphasizing the
effect of societal attitudes toward the
crime on the handling of rape cases by
medical and law enforcement personnel, and
by the courts. The significance of

popular and widely accepted myths about
rape and racist prejudices are also
explored.

120. Goldner, Norman S. "Rape as a Heinous But
      Understudied Offense." THE JOURNAL OF
      CRIMINAL LAW, CRIMINOLOGY, AND POLICE
      SCIENCE, 63(3): 402-407, 1972.

      Goldner examines available data concerning
      rape in an attempt to discover why rape,
      universally regarded as a serious offense,
      is virtually unstudied. The frequency,
      time, location, and methods used for a
      crime of rape to be committed are discussed
      in detail. Victim and offender character-
      istics are also presented, and the
      psychology of the rapist is explored. The
      article concludes with observations
      made by the author in an attempt to explain
      the lack of research and study on the
      subject of rape.

121. Goldstein, Allan. "Corroboration in Rape
      Cases in New York--A Half Step Forward."
      ALBANY LAW REVIEW, 37: 306-328, 1973.

      The 1972 statute requiring corroboration
      in sexual offense cases in New York State
      is discussed. The actual statute is
      described and explained in detail.
      Sections of the New York State Penal Code
      which dealt with the prosecution of sexual
      offenses prior to the enactment of the
      1972 statute are discussed in order to
      explain the changes in the law as a
      result of the new statute, and comparisons
      are made between prior statutes and the
      new law. In an historical analysis,
      Goldstein points out the elements of
      sexual offenses thought to need corroboration,
      concluding that no element of the crime of
      rape could be proven without additional
      evidence to support the testimony of the
      victim. However, two primary elements of
      a rape complaint were thought to require
      additional evidence: the identity of the
      assailant, and the fact that a rape had
      actually been committed. The effect of

required corroboration on other offenses committed with the rape is analyzed. Goldstein identifies two obvious problems with the statutes governing sexual offenses prior to the enactment of the 1972 statute: the statutory need for corroboration in sexual crimes, and the judicial "doctrine of circumvention" which developed from this need. Each problem is discussed in detail, and legislative attempts to reform the sources of these problems are presented. This article concludes with a discussion of the problems remaining after the enactment of the 1972 corroboration requirement. The author states that the amount of corroborating evidence necessary to sustain a conviction for rape should be in proportion to the degree of improbability existing in the victim's testimony.

122. Goldstein, Michael J. "Exposure to Erotic Stimuli and Sexual Deviance." JOURNAL OF SOCIAL ISSUES, 29(3): 197-219, 1973.

The author relates the findings of a study developed to assess whether a relationship exists between a person's experience with pornography and his choice of a mode for sexual expression. Samples were drawn of convicted sexual offenders, people from the general community, heavy users of pornography, and sexual deviants. The extent of the use of pornography by each group was examined to ascertain experiences with pornography during adolescence and during adulthood. The findings of this study suggest that sexual arousal following exposure to pornography does not cause a person to act in a certain way sexually. The choice of a mode for sexual expression is influenced by the availability of a partner, and a person's own attitudes toward sexuality.

123. Goodman, G.R. "Proposed Amendments to the
     Criminal Code With Respect to the
     Victims of Rape and Related Sexual
     Offenses." MANITOBA LAW JOURNAL,
     6: 275-281, 1975.

The author supports the proposal to
amend the Canadian Criminal Code in
regard to the crime of rape. The
proposed amendments would limit the
cross-examination of the victim to
material which is directly relevant to
the present case. This would prohibit
the admission of a woman's past sexual
history into evidence unless the
information is required to impeach the
credibility of the victim, or where the
victim's character is directly relevant
to the case. Goodman presents a portion
of a trial transcript from a rape case
to illustrate his position. He
concludes by stating that community
attitudes toward rape cannot be
changed overnight, implying that
these attitudes may influence the
decision as to the admissibility of
details of a victim's private life into
evidence at a rape trial.

124. Gordon, Gary. "What Constitutes Rape."
     VALOR, 16: 16-20, 1965.

This article centers around the diversity
of legal definitions for the crime of
rape. Gordon discusses statutory and
common law definitions, and provides
many examples to illustrate various
definitions. Examples are also provided
which do not support the popular
conception of the rapist as a sexual
psychopath. Criteria for determining an
act to be statutory rape is discussed,
in addition to punishments for rape as
required by law in various states.
Gordon concludes that the determination
of a crime as rape rests in the hands of
the jury, and is based upon information
given to the jury by the attorneys involved
in the case, and by the judge.

125. Graham, Loral. "Defend Yourself!" THE
CANADIAN NURSE, 64(8): 38-41, August 1968.

Although written specifically for nurses,
the precautions and methods of self-
defense presented in this article are
applicable to all women under many
circumstances. Graham presents
statistics concerning the increasing
crime rate, and the susceptibility of
women to violent crime. Methods for
protecting one's self at home, in a car,
or on the street are discussed. The
author explains ways in which a woman
can fight an assailant with simple things
usually in her possession, such as her
fingernails, a lighted cigarette, or an
umbrella.

126. Gramont, Sache de and Nancy R. deGramont.
"Rape, True and False." VOGUE, 152:
108-109, 155-157, June 1971.

Each author discusses rape from a
different perspective. Sache deGramont
views rape and courtship as seeking the
same goal, with the primary difference
being the method with which that goal is
achieved. In addition to forcible,
physical rape, symbolic, metaphorical,
and attempted rape are also discussed.
The author defines rape as "the specific
masculine crime," stating that by making
a woman feel guilty for being the victim
of a rape, men may be refusing to accept
the collective responsibility for the
conduct of all rapists.

The perspective of Nancy deGramont is
somewhat different. She discusses the
process of socializing children into sex
roles and the consequences of society's
conversion of sex into status. The
significance of women seeking protection
from men, and the relationship between
aggression and protection are explored.
The author feels that, "We consent to a
society that gives us roles with
consequences of which we are largely
unaware," and rape is a perfect example
of these consequences.

127. Graves, Lester R. and J.T. Francisco.
     "Medico-Legal Aspects of Rape."
     MEDICAL ASPECTS OF HUMAN SEXUALITY,
     4(4): 109-120, April 1970.

     The importance of medical evidence to the
     conviction or acquittal of an alleged
     rapist is central to this article. Graves
     and Francisco describe in detail the
     collection, testing, and recording of
     the evidence, and briefly outline
     procedures for medically treating the
     victim of a sexual assault. Also discussed
     is the patient's emotional condition
     immediately following the assault, and
     possible psychological repercussions of the
     crime.

128. Greer, Germaine. "Seduction is a Four-Letter
     Word." in: Schultz, LeRoy, editor, RAPE
     VICTIMOLOGY. Springfield, Illinois:
     Charles C. Thomas, 1975, pp. 374-395.

     In spite of the understanding by many
     men in our culture that a woman cannot
     be raped unless she wants to be, many
     women greatly fear the threat of rape.
     Greer discusses many forms of rape,
     including what she terms "petty rapes"
     and "rape by fraud," in which there is
     no complaint made to the legal authorities.
     The difficulty of getting convictions for
     rape is also mentioned during a brief
     discussion of the legal aspects of sexual
     assaults. The dating ritual in modern
     society is explored as a battleground for
     different forms of rape and exploitation.
     The author concludes with a feminist
     statement concerning the weapons a woman
     has at her disposal for fighting
     exploitation and rape.

129. Griffin, Susan. "Rape: The All-American
     Crime." RAMPARTS, 10: 26-35, September
     1971.

     The author states that women are always
     aware of the possibility of rape, and
     that in spite of myths to the contrary,
     they fear it. This fear of rape is

supported by the widely held belief that
rape is natural behavior. In comparing
this notion with ideas about rape held
by other cultures, anthropoligists
and sociologists conclude that most
rapes which occur in our culture are
planned rather than the result of
impulsive, instinctive behavior. Thus,
rape is learned behavior and thought to
be "understandable" behavior by our
culture, although it is prohibited by
law. Aggressive behavior is as expected
of the male as passive behavior is
of the female. One of the most common
rape myths revolves around this concept,
believing that women seal their fate by
their passivity--indeed, women are
thought to secretly desire and enjoy
rape, and actually encourage their
assailants. Griffin feels that a male
dominated society rewards aggressive,
sexual behavior. Men define standards of
"chastity" and women who do not conform
to these standards are candidates for
rape. In other words, rape keeps women
in their place. Griffin also explores
laws governing rape, stating that rape
laws protect the rights of men as
possessors of women and reinforce the
idea that rape is a crime committed by
men, against men--women as rape victims
are only instruments.

130.   "Guidelines for the Interview and Examination
        of Alleged Rape Victims: A Conjoint Effort
        of the California Medical Association
        Committee on Evolving Trends in Society
        Affecting Life, and the Advisory Panels
        of Obstetrics and Gynecology, Pathology,
        and Psychiatry of the Scientific Board
        of the California Medical Association."
        THE WESTERN JOURNAL OF MEDICINE, 123(5):
        420-422, November 1975.

        The importance of sympathetic medical
        treatment for the rape victim's
        psychological, as well as physical,
        health is emphasized. These guidelines
        encompass four primary areas of treatment

for rape victims; adequate information
on the assault and the victim's medical
history, consent of the victim for the
examination, the examination itself,
and the victim's psychological evironment.
Procedures for medical personnel in
treating the victim during each area of
treatment are explained in detail.

131.   Haas, Karl.   "Rape: New Perspectives and New
       Approaches." THE PROSECUTOR, 11(5):
       357-359, 1976.

       The District Attorney's office in
       Multnomah County, Oregon created a
       program to deal with rape victims.
       The program, The District Attorney's
       Rape Victim Advocate Program, set goals
       for itself: to prevent rape, to increase
       the number of reported rapes and rape
       convictions, and to increase community
       awareness concerning rape and rape
       victims.   The structure and operation
       of the program is discussed, emphasizing
       the importance of sympathetic treatment
       for the rape victim.

132.   Haines, E.L.   "The Character of the Rape
       Victim." CHITTY'S LAW JOURNAL, 23(2):
       57-59, 1975.

       During a rape trial, the victim actually
       finds herself on trial.   Victims are
       frequently asked questions of a personal
       nature which are not directly relevant to
       the case being considered by the court.
       Haines attributes this situation to the
       fact that the laws governing rape were
       conceived and are administered by men
       who have not been victims of rape.
       Safeguards enacted by the Canadian
       courts to protect crime victims,
       particularly victims of rape, are
       discussed, stressing the importance of
       the trial judge's discretion in allowing
       evidence to be admitted and certain forms
       of questioning to be conducted.   Haines
       concludes by stating that a rape victim

should be advised of her rights as
a witness, and should have the right
to retain counsel for herself if she
so desires, as guarenteed by the Canadian
Bill of Rights.

133. Halleck, Seymour L. "Emotional Effects of
Victimization." in: Slovenko,Ralph,
editor, SEXUAL BEHAVIOR AND THE LAW.
Springfield, Illinois: Charles C.
Thomas, publisher, 1965, pp. 673-686.

Sexual assault leaves invisible emotional
scars on its victims. When this selection
was written, the focus of society's
interest was on the offender in a rape,
frequently at the expense of the victim.
Consequently, the victim's emotional
needs often went unattended. Halleck
discusses the psychological trauma
experienced by victims of sex crimes,
and points out certain problems which
are directly related to the victim's
age and existing personality problems.
The victim-offender relationship is
considered to be a very important factor
in the degree of psychological trauma
experienced by the victim. The
author recommends that scientific studies
be conducted in order to better understand
the causes of sex offenses and the effect
of the crimes upon the victims.

134. Hanss, Joseph W. "Another Look at the Care
of the Rape Victim." ARIZONA MEDICINE,
32(8): 634-635, August 1975.

Hanss states that the rape victim is
often treated impersonally, coldly, and
inhumanly by hospital personnel.
Although victims of rape respond to the
assault in different ways, the
immediate reaction in most women is the
fear of being killed by their assailants.
In order to aid the victim with her
adjustment problems following the
assault, assault crisis centers have been
established all over the country. In

many juristictions, law enforcement
agencies have developed similar programs
which are staffed by personnel with
special training, who are sensitive to
the psychological and emotional needs of
the rape victim. In addition to
discussing these special treatment
programs, Hanss provides a detailed
explanation of procedures followed
during the medical examination of a
rape victim.

135. Harris, Lucy Reed. "Towards a Consent Standard
      in the Law of Rape." UNIVERSITY OF
      CHICAGO LAW REVIEW, 43(3): 613-645,
      Spring 1976.

      Harris states that although the most
      important element necessary to prove rape
      in a court of law is non-consent on the
      part of the victim, the law has not
      developed a uniform, effective consent
      standard. The purposes of enacting
      rape laws and the actual practice of
      these laws are discussed, including the
      controversies surrounding the
      formulation of definitions of rape,
      and in the admissibility of certain
      forms of evidence during a rape trial.
      Arguements concerning the meaning of
      non-consent in rape cases are presented,
      and consent issues in other areas of
      the law are compared with the issue of
      consent in rape laws. The author
      concludes that consent standards for
      rape cases should be consistent with the
      consent standards operating in other
      areas of the law.

136. Hartwig, Patricia A. and Georgette Bennett
      Sandler. "Rape Victims: Reasons,
      Responses, and Reforms." INTELLECT,
      103(2366): 507-511, May-June 1975.

      Hartwig and Sandler focus on the
      sociological and legal aspects of rape.
      The cultural context in which rape
      occurs is examined, emphasizing the

development of sex-role stereotypes.
The dehumanization and alienation which
results from the perpetuation of these
stereotypes leads to a hostility which
may eventually lead to aggressive
behaviors, such as rape. Attitudes
concerning male/female relationships,
roles, and positions in society are
said to be instrumental determinants
of the response given rape victims by
social service agencies and by the
public. Concerning the law, the authors
state that the legal system is
dominated by male attitudes and a male
value system. The stringent corroboration
requirements applicable in some states
are discussed as reflections of these
attitudes which question the credibility
of the victim. States that have initiated
legislative reform to eliminate some
of the problems inherent in existing rape
laws are also explored. The authors
conclude by discussing the need for
improved treatment of rape victims,
programs for controlling or preventing
rape, and the incidence and extent of
rape in this country.

137. Hayman, Charles R. "Increasing Rape Reflects
        Increasing Violence." SEXUAL BEHAVIOR,
        1(8): 33, November 1971.

        Commenting on Menachem Amir's article,
        "Forcible Rape," which also appears in
        this issue of SEXUAL BEHAVIOR, Hayman
        states that violent crimes in general
        have increased considerably since
        Amir's study in 1965. Noting that
        although his own study of rape in
        Washington D.C., still in progress at
        the time of this article, supplements
        Amir's study, Hayman cites a few
        significant differences in the findings
        of the two studies. Sociological,
        psychological, and medical aspects of
        the Washington, D.C. study are discussed
        and compared or contrasted with Amir's
        Philadelphia study. Hayman emphasizes
        the importance of emotional support for

the victims of forcible rape, and the
need for changes in rape laws and court
procedures which defend the offender
at the expense of the victim.

138. Hayman, Charles R. and Celso-Ramon Garcia.
       "Emergency Department Protocol for
       Management of Rape Cases." JOURNAL OF
       THE AMERICAN MEDICAL ASSOCIATION, 226(13):
       1577-1578, December 24-31, 1973.

       Hayman and Garcia each discuss procedures
       for handling rape cases in the emergency
       room of a typical hospital. The
       procedure for examining the sexual
       assault victim is described in detail,
       and the risk of pregnancy and gonorrhea
       for the victim is discussed.

139. Hayman, Charles R. and Charlene Lanza.
       "Sexual Assault on Women and Girls."
       AMERICAN JOURNAL OF OBSTETRICS AND
       GYNECOLOGY, 109(3): 480-486,
       February 1971.

       Police referrals of sexual assault victims
       in the District of Columbia to hospitals
       may occur because the victim is in need
       of emergency medical care, or because
       medical evidence must be collected to
       ascertain the nature of the alleged
       assault. The authors collected data
       concerning alleged sexual assaults referred
       to a large metropolitan hospital over a
       one year period. The age distribution,
       race, and specific injuries of the victims
       were noted. An increase in the number of
       victims referred to health department
       clinics for treatment and re-examination
       following the assault was observed. The
       authors state that the examination of a
       sexual assault victim should be performed
       by a trained physician away from the
       actual emergency room setting, and that
       special attention should be given to the
       victim's emotional condition.

140. Hayman, Charles R. and Charlene Lanza.
      "Victimology of Sexual Assault."
      MEDICAL ASPECTS OF HUMAN SEXUALITY,
      5(10): 152-161, October 1971.

      As the title suggests, this article
      focuses on the victim of a sexual
      assault. The subjects of this study
      were eight women who had been treated
      at the District of Columbia General
      Hospital (Washington, D.C.) for
      injuries received during sexual assaults.
      Details of each case, including
      complications (physical, emotional, and
      social) and treatment, are presented.
      The authors emphasize the importance of
      emotional support for the victim by
      the hospital staff, in addition to
      immediate, expert, physical examination
      and treatment.

141. Hayman, Charles R. and others. "A Public
      Health Program for Sexually Assaulted
      Females." PUBLIC HEALTH REPORTS,
      82(6): 497-504, June 1967.

      The District of Columbia Department of
      Public Health established a treatment
      program to provide emergency treatment
      for victims of rape. In addition to
      treating the victim's immediate needs,
      the program directs referrals and offers
      a public health nurse follow-up service.
      The authors discuss the procedures
      followed by program personnel in handling
      a rape complaint. The complaints
      received during a nine-month period were
      studied and the findings of the study
      are reported in detail. A very brief
      review of the medical literature
      published on rape is also provided.

69

142. Hayman, Charles R. and others. "Rape and Its
         Consequences." MEDICAL ASPECTS OF
         HUMAN SEXUALITY, 6(2): 12-31, February 1972.

         Hayman discusses rape, in a question and
         answer format, with six professionals
         from the legal and medical fields.
         Topics discussed include the incidence
         of rape in this country, precautionary
         measures for preventing rape,
         characteristics of rapists, medical
         procedure followed in examining and
         treating rape victims, and police
         procedures for dealing with rape cases.
         In his closing remarks, Hayman emphasizes
         the importance of emotional support for
         rape victims, and suggests ways of
         minimizing the victim's emotional trauma
         following the assault.

143. Hayman, Charles R. and others. "Rape in the
         District of Columbia." AMERICAN
         JOURNAL OF OBSTRETRICS AND GYNECOLOGY,
         113: 91-97, May 1, 1972.

         The authors examined records of female
         victims of sexual assault treated at
         D.C. General Hospital (Washington, D.C.)
         over an eighteen-month period. They
         then grouped the subjects according
         to the age and race of the victim and
         the assailant, the relationship of
         the victim to the offender, the time
         of the assault, the location of the
         assault, and the injuries and
         subsequent treatment received by the
         victim. The authors discuss these
         patterns and compare them with the
         patterns identified in an earlier study
         conducted by them.

144. Hayman, Charles R. and others. "Sexual Assault
         on Women and Children in the District
         of Columbia." PUBLIC HEALTH REPORTS,
         83(12): 1021-1028, December 1968.

         The authors studied four hundred forty-
         eight (448) cases of alleged sexual assault,
         which had been referred to the District
         of Columbia General Hospital by the
         Metropolitan Police Department over a

period of one year. Methods of immediate
and long-range medical and psychiatric
treatment are briefly described. In
examining the records from cases of alleged
rape, the authors grouped the cases according
to the race and age of the victim, finding
that the victims ranged in age from one
to eighty-eight years, with fifty-eight
percent (58%) of the victims being under
seventeen years of age. In regard to
race, eighty-seven percent (87%) of the
victims were non-white. In speaking of
race, however, it must be noted that the
ratio of non-white to white in the general
population was three to one. The type of
sexual contact, the amount of force used
in the assault, and the probability that
the assault had occurred as alleged were
among the variables examined. These
variables were also compared using the
race and age of the victims as a basis
for comparison. The relationship
between the victim and the offender, and
the location of the offense (the victim's
home, the offender's home, or elsewhere)
were also identified. The authors
conclude that seventy-five percent (75%)
of the incidents of alleged vaginal
penetration had occurred as claimed by
the victims, and that most of the assaults
had occurred in either the victims' or
the offenders' homes. The highest incidence
of rape accompanied by some form of "bodily
harm" occurred most frequently in white
victims in the eighteen to twenty-four
year old age group, while the lowest rate
of reported rape came from victims over
twenty-four years of age.

145. Hayman, Charles R. and others. "What to Do
      For Victims of Rape." RESIDENT AND
      STAFF PHYSICIAN, pp. 29-32, August 1973.

      Recognizing the need for improved methods
      of treatment for rape victims, the District
      of Columbia Department of Human Resources
      and the Metropolitan Police Department
      developed a treatment program. The
      development and operation of the program

are discussed in detail. The authors emphasize the need for specially trained and experienced personnel on duty in the hospital's emergency room to insure complete and careful examinations of alleged sexual assault victims. The medical concerns of victims immediately following a sexual assault are identified and methods for treating them are presented. The authors conclude by emphasizing the extent of emotional damage to the rape victim and the need for understanding responses from the people she comes in contact with immediately following the assault.

146. Healthwitches. "Forcible Rape." OFF OUR BACKS, 2(7): 8-9, March 1972.

The authors present methods for preventing rape and advise women to think about what they would do in a situation where they may be victims of rape. If a woman is raped, she must decide whether to report the crime to the police. A discussion of police procedure for forcible rape cases is presented, including guidelines for the gathering of evidence. The typical medical examination given to rape victims is described, and the dangers of venereal disease and pregnancy are discussed. The article concludes with a proposal for the establishment of a rape crisis center.

147. "A Healthy Rise in Rape." NEWSWEEK, 80(5): 72, July 31, 1972.

The Federal Bureau of Investigation's Uniform Crime Reports show a substantial rise in rapes reported to law enforcement agencies. The major reason given for the increase is the victim's willingness to go to the police and talk about the crime. It is noted, however, that the increase in the number of reported rapes does not indicate that there has been an increase in the actual number of rapes committed.

148. Heimel, Cyndy. "I Should Have Known: It's August." MAJORITY REPORT, 4(9): 1, August 22, 1974.

Heimel states that the highest incidence of rape occurs during the month of August. Following a brief account of a rape related incident experienced by the author, a program organized by some feminist groups in New York City to aid in the prevention of rape is discussed. The women developed a program designed to increase public awareness of the problem of rape and to urge the implementation of specific educational and preventive services.

149. Hibey, Richard A. "The Trial of a Rape Case: An Advocate's Analysis of Corroboration, Consent, and Character." AMERICAN CRIMINAL LAW REVIEW, 11:309-334, 1973.

As indicated by the title, the author discusses, in detail, the three primary areas in which the victim's credibility is frequently questioned during a rape trial. Regarding corroboration, Hibey explores the problems involved in the identification of the assailant. The role of the prosecutor in the corroboration of an identification, the evidence necessary to prove penetration, the defense attorney's inquiry into the evidence corroborating an identification, and other issues involved in corroboration are discussed. The question of consent is an important one in a rape case. Hibey emphasizes the importance of a strong defense to the issue of consent. The defense attorney, in proving consent, legitimizes and decriminalizes the act. The question of a victim's prior sexual history is a controversal one. Testimony concerning a victim's prior sexual history is often admissible as evidence during a rape trial if the defense attorney uses it in an effort to prove consent in the case. Hibey discusses

the use of evidence pertaining to the
victim's character, including the admission
of testimony by "character witnesses."
Some popular myths concerning rape, which
may act to influence the decision of a
jury, are also presented.

150. Hicks, Dorothy J. and Charlotte R. Platt.
      "Medical Treatment of the Victim: The
      Development of a Rape Treatment Center."
      in: Walker, Marcia J. and Stanley L.
      Brodsky, editors, SEXUAL ASSAULT.
      Lexington, Massachusetts: Lexington Books,
      1976, pp. 53-59.

      The establishment of a rape treatment
      center in Dade County, Florida, and its
      subsequent methods of operation, are
      discussed in detail. The center treats
      all victims of sexual assaults, both male
      and female. The functions of the center,
      operating procedures for the physicians,
      nurses, and counselors on the staff, and the
      cooperation of the police are explored.
      Hicks and Platt conclude by describing the
      effect of the treatment center on the
      community. The attitudes of the police,
      court personnel, and the public are
      changing and becoming more sensitive to
      the problem of rape, and, consequently,
      the rape laws of Florida have been reformed.

151. Hilberman, Elaine. "Rape: The Ultimate
      Violation of Self." AMERICAN JOURNAL OF
      PSYCHIATRY, 133(4): 436-437, April 1976.

      Hilberman briefly comments on four articles
      also published in this issue of AMERICAN
      JOURNAL OF PSYCHIATRY, in addition to
      discussing the crime of rape from an
      empathic, feminist perspective. She
      touches upon society's double standard
      in her discussion by saying that,
      according to the myths promulgated by
      society, a sexually experienced woman
      cannot be raped unless she wants to be.
      Thus, the victim is thought to be the
      responsible party in cases of rape.

The humiliation and sense of powerlessness
that is felt by the rape victim are central
to Hilberman's discussion. Eradication
of rape, states Hilberman, is contingent
upon a redefinition of sex roles and the
elimination of the stereotypes of the
sexually aggressive, powerful man and the
submissive woman.

152. Hodges, E.J. and others. "The Offense of Rape
in Victoria." AUSTRALIAN AND NEW
ZEALAND JOURNAL OF CRIMINOLOGY, 5(4):
225-240, December 1972.

This article discusses the findings of a
study on rape conducted by four university
students. Variables studied in connection
with the offenders included marital status,
education, family background, sexual
attitudes and experience, mental health,
and prior convictions. Victim
characteristics are not discussed in
detail. Concerning the offenses themselves,
the location of the offense, the degree
of consent or resistance demonstrated by
the victim, and the amount of violence
and force used are explored. Rape laws
in the United States and in Australia,
and the criteria utilized in each country
for the sentencing of rape offenders
are thoroughly discussed. Recommendations
for reform are also suggested.

153. Holmstrom, Lynda Lytle and Ann Wolbert Burgess.
"Rape: The Victim and the Criminal Justice
System." INTERNATIONAL JOURNAL OF
CRIMINOLOGY AND PENOLOGY, 3(2): 101-110,
May 1975.

The focus of this article is the point that
the victim of a rape is often treated as
the criminal. The victim, then, faces
two periods of crisis: the actual rape,
and her contact with the criminal justice
system. The authors illustrate this
point by relating the findings of their
own study of rape victims in a large city,
who had reported rapes to the police and
had followed through with each stage of

criminal justice processing. Beginning
with the victim's decision to report the
crime, Holmstrom and Burgess follow
the victim through the actual reporting
of the rape to the police, interrogation
by the police, the victim's decision
to prosecute her assailant, and, finally,
focus on the trial itself.

154. Holmstrom, Lynda Lytle and Ann Wolbert Burgess.
       "Rape: The Victim Goes on Trial."
       in: Drapkin, Israel and Emilio Viano,
       VICTIMOLOGY: A NEW FOCUS, Volume III.
       Lexington, Massachusetts: Lexington Books,
       1975, pp. 31-47.

       In a rape trial, the man is, technically,
       the only person on trial. The authors
       point out that, in reality, the victim
       is also on trial, and that she is often
       treated as if she had committed a crime.
       Tactics employed by the defense attorney
       in an effort to show that the victim is
       responsible for the crime are explored.
       These tactics include submitting a woman's
       past sexual history into evidence and
       showing that the victim did not struggle
       sufficiently and, therefore, consented
       to the act. The authors state that
       evidence, corroborated or uncorroborated,
       can be interpreted in different ways,
       and conviction for rape depends on the
       way in which the jury chooses to interpret
       the evidence presented to them.

155. Hooper, Anthony. "Fraud in Assault and Rape."
       UNIVERSITY OF BRITISH COLUMBIA LAW
       REVIEW, 3(2): 117-130, May 1968.

       According to the Canadian Criminal Code,
       if a woman is forced to consent to sexual
       intercourse through fraudulent means, the
       resulting act may be considered rape.
       Consent obtained through fraudulent means
       includes: misrepresentation of the motive
       behind the act, submission of the victim
       to the act when the nature of the act
       was not understood by the victim, sexual
       gratification achieved under the guise
       of medical treatment, and impersonation

of a spouse. Through the use of examples
from actual cases, Hooper discusses the
obtaining of consent by various fraudulent
means. Focusing on one particular case,
the author argues that the question of the
"nature and quality" of an act is ambiguous,
and it is difficult to pass judgement on
a case of alleged fraud.

156. Horin, Adele. "Rape: How Women Can Stop It."
PAGEANT, **pp.** 61-66, February 1975.

Horin emphasizes the importance of the
women's movement in restoring women's
confidence in their abilities to do
something to prevent rape. Self defense
is considered to be an individual question
and dependent on the circumstances of
the particular assault. The difficulty
in obtaining convictions for rape is also
discussed, noting the underlying
assumption during a rape trial that the
victim and the defendant are equally
guilty in a rape situation. It is this
assumption that is providing the impetus
for women to take action directed at
reforming the rape laws and the criminal
justice system. In conclusion, programs
developed to assist the rape victim
immediately following the assault are
described.

157. Horos, Carol V. RAPE. New Canaan, Connecticut:
Tobey Publishing Company, Inc., 1974.
130 pages.

This book explores every aspect of the crime
of rape. The characteristics of the offender
and the victim, the history of rape and
rape laws, ways to prevent the crime,
reporting the crime, medical treatment,
court procedures and the trial itself,
and emotional support and help for
the victims are the major areas discussed.
Horos outlines procedures and suggests
guidelines for establishing a rape crisis
center, and a listing of rape crisis
centers across the country is provided.

158. "How They Help Rape Victims at the University
     of Chicago." RESIDENT AND STAFF PHYSICIAN,
     p. 31, August 1973.

     The emergency room of the Billings Hospital
     at the University of Chicago has developed
     a specialized routine for treating the
     physical and emotional needs of the rape
     victim immediately following the assault.
     The unique feature of this treatment
     procedure is that it utilizes the services
     of a chaplain in every case. The procedure
     is described in detail, emphasizing the
     role of the chaplain in this particular
     treatment process.

159. "I Never Set Out to Rape Anybody . . . ."
     MS. MAGAZINE, 1: 22-23, December 1972.

     A rapist discusses the motivation behind
     his offense. In his particular case, the
     portrayal of men and women in movies and
     television created an idealistic image
     of masculinity. In an attempt to approach
     this ideal, the author was compelled to
     engage in violent sexual behavior. He
     states that the common image of
     masculinity in this society is a violent,
     hypersexual one, and that this image is
     perpetuated through the media.

160. "I Was raped." COSMOPOLITAN, 167(1): 34-38,
     July 1969.

     A rape victim provides a detailed
     personal account of her experience,
     including the medical and legal
     processing involved in her case. In
     addition, suggestions are made for
     securing one's house or apartment against
     intrusion.

161. "If She Consented Once, She Consented Again--
     A Legal Fallacy in Forcible Rape Cases."
     VALPARAISO UNIVERSITY LAW REVIEW,
     10: 127-167, 1976.

     This article discusses the effect on the
     court of admitting a woman's prior
     consensual sexual history into evidence

during a rape trial. Current legislation
governing the admissibility of a victim's
past sexual history into evidence is
examined and the types of evidence
concerning the victim's past sexual behavior
typically admitted during a rape trial is
analyzed. After exploring the relevance
of a complainant's prior sexual history
to a rape case, it is concluded that
much of this evidence is not directly
relevant and should not be considered
admissible as evidence.

162. Jarrett, Tommy W. "Criminal Law--Psychiatric
Examination of Prosecutrix in Rape Case."
NORTH CAROLINA LAW REVIEW, 45: 234-240,
1966.

In most juristictions, the verdict in a
rape case is based on either the
uncorroborated testimony of the victim
or, in cases where the victim's credibility
is in question, the testimony of someone
other than the prosecutrix in corroboration.
In addition, other jurisdictions completely
reject the common law rule of convicting
a defendant on only the uncorroborated
testimony of the victim, and require,
by statute or by judicial decision,
corroborating evidence to prove that a
rape has been committed. An alternative
to these rules has been proposed which
requires the prosecutrix in a rape case
to submit to a psychiatric examination
before the trial begins. The purpose
of this examination is to determine
whether the victim suffers from a mental
or emotional condition which may affect
her ability to give truthful testimony
during the trial. Jarrett discusses the
propriety of such an examination by
referring to three court cases in which
the proper use of a psychiatric examination
of the prosecutrix was questioned.

163. Jesse, Franklin C. "Criteria for Commitment
     Under the Wisconsin Sex Crimes Act."
     WISCONSIN LAW REVIEW, 1967: 980-987,
     Fall 1967.

   Under the Wisconsin Sex Crimes Act, a
   person convicted of a serious sexual
   offense is referred to the Department
   of Health and Social Services for a
   pre-sentence investigation. The
   Department recommends either commitment
   to a treatment facility or sentencing
   by the criminal court on the basis of
   this investigation. Prior to 1967, the
   Department's recommendation required a
   mandatory commitment of the offender, and
   the court was unable to alter this
   recommendation. In 1967, the commitment
   decision was left up to the trial judge
   as a result of a controversial court case,
   and not to the Department of Health and
   Social Services. Jesse discusses the
   criterion for commitment as required by
   the Wisconsin statute, and suggests
   priorities for making a decision to
   commit a sex offender for treatment.

164. Johnson, Edwinna G. "Evidence--Rape Trials--
     Victim's Prior Sexual History." BAYLOR
     LAW REVIEW, 27(2): 362-369, Spring 1975.

   A Texas law allowing the victim's prior
   sexual history to be admitted as evidence
   in a rape trial, if it is deemed relevant
   to an issue in the case by the judge, is
   the subject of this article. The law
   under discussion is a revision of a
   previous law allowing the admissability
   of evidence concerning the victim's
   prior sexual history to help prove that
   the victim had consented to sexual
   intercourse with the defendant. In
   conclusion, Johnson states that the
   revision is an important step away from
   giving the defendant an advantage
   during the trial, by causing the victim
   to be treated as if she were the defendant,
   and towards a greater number of successful
   rape prosecutions.

165. Jones, Cathaleene and Elliot Aronson.
"Attribution of Fault to a Rape Victim
as a Function of Respectability of the
Victim." JOURNAL OF PERSONALITY AND
SOCIAL PSYCHOLOGY, 26(3): 415-419, 1973.

The authors hypothesized that more
responsibility for a rape is attributed
to a victim if the victim is a married
woman or a virgin than if she is a
divorcee. To test this hypothesis,
two hundred thirty-four (234)
undergraduate students were given
varied accounts of rape situations in
which the victim was either a virgin,
a married woman, or a divorcee. The
study showed that more respectibility
was attributed to the virgin or to the
married woman than to the divorcee, and,
in the case of rape, less fault for the
crime was attributed to the victim if
she was a divorcee rather than a virgin
or a married woman. Regarding the sentencing
of a convicted rapist, the study showed
that the degree of respectibility attributed
to the victim influenced the severity of
sentence.

166. Kardener, Sheldon H. "Rape Fantasies."
JOURNAL OF RELIGION AND HEALTH, 14(1):
50-57, 1975.

Kardener focuses on the psychology of the
rape fantasy. The terms "rape" and
"fantasy" are defined, and an introduction
to the psychological development of a
person, especially the development of
sexuality and aggressivity, is provided.
In discussing sexual functioning and its
relationship to sexual roles, the author
views the fantasy to rape as a desire to
dominate and associates this desire with
a "grown-up" child's game model. The
influence of parental attitudes toward
sex and the effect of role models on
sexuality and the development of rape
fantasies are also explored.

167. Keefe, Mary L. and Henry T. O'Reilly.
"Attitudinal Training for Police and
Emergency Room Personnel." THE POLICE
CHIEF, 42(11): 36-37, November 1975.

The period of crisis experienced by most sex
crime victims is complicated by feelings
of guilt, shame, and embarassment. The
pressure felt by the rape victim immediately
following the assault may influence her
willingness to cooperate with law enforcement
personnel. The Sex Crimes Analysis Unit
of the New York City Police Department
recognized the need for a positive change
in the attitudes of medical and law
enforcement personnel, in order to
encourage the complete cooperation of the
rape victim in reporting the crime and
providing information during the subsequent
investigation. It was felt that a
sensitive, non-judgemental response from
the police would definitely be to the
advantage of the victim and of the police
department. Specific training in crisis
intervention and anxiety-reducing techniques
was initiated into the police training
program. The authors cite statistics to
illustrate the success of this program.
Implications for the implementation of
such a program for hospital personnel
is also discussed.

168. Keefe, Mary L. and Henry T. O"Reilly.
"Changing Perspectives in Sex Crimes
Investigations." in: Walker, Marcia J.
and Stanley L. Brodsky, editors, SEXUAL
ASSAULT. Lexington, Massachusetts:
Lexington Books, 1976, pp. 161-168.

The investigation procedure employed by
the police for sex crimes in New York
City is discussed. The training program
for sex crimes investigators involved
the learning of investigation techniques
and crisis intervention techniques. There
was also an attempt to change the attitudes
of the potential sex crimes investigators
in order to make them more aware of the
psychological trauma and feelings of the
victim. The authors conclude that the

program is very successful, and note th
arrests for forcible rape have increased
significantly as a result of the
implementation of the program. They
suggest that other law enforcement agencie
include the use of crisis intervention
techniques in their training programs
for sex crimes investigators.

169. Keefe, Mary L. and Henry T. O'Reilly.
"Developing a Pertinent Rape Prevention
Lecture Program." LAW AND ORDER,
24(3): 64-67, March 1976.

Keefe and O'Reilly present the standard
lecture on rape prevention, which had
been developed by the Sex Crimes Analysis
Unit of the New York City Police Department.
Prevention is emphasized as the best defense
against assault. The lecture includes
methods of securing one's home and car
against intrusion, and tips for the
woman walking alone.

170. Keefe, Mary L. and Henry T. O'Reilly.
"The Police and the Rape Victim in New
York." VICTIMOLOGY: AN INTERNATIONAL
JOURNAL, 1(2): 272-283, Summer 1976.

The establishment and operation of the Sex
Crimes Analysis Unit of the New York City
Police Department is the focus of this
article. Recognizing the need for
sensitivity to the needs of the victim
when processing rape complaints, the Sex
Crimes Analysis Unit is staffed by female
investigators. It was expected that the
presence of female investigators would
encourage victims to report sex crimes to
the police. To emphasize the need for
personnel who are sensitive to the rape
victim's situation, the authors present
the details of three case studies which
illustrate the frequent insensitivity
of police and medical personnel. As a
result of the development of the unit,
victims are receiving sympathic attention
from the unit's personnel, as is illustrated

by additional case studies. Keefe and
O'Reilly state that the responses from
the victims and the general public to
the work of the unit have been very
positive.

171. Kercher, Glen A. and C. Eugene Walker.
      "Reactions of Convicted Rapists to
      Sexually Explicit Stimuli." JOURNAL OF
      ABNORMAL PSYCHOLOGY, 81(1): 46-50,
      February 1973.

      Various studies have been conducted in
      order to ascertain the effect of pornography
      upon the commission of sexual crimes.
      Kercher and Walker, after reviewing some
      of these studies and their findings,
      conclude that the literature has failed
      to demonstrate a significant relationship
      between the commission of sex crimes
      and pornography. To determine whether
      convicted rapists experience a greater,
      or less, degree of physiological arousal
      to pornographic material than do men
      convicted of other crimes, the authors
      conducted an experiment with adult offenders
      from the Texas Department of Corrections.
      The subjects were shown sexually explicit
      slides, and their reactions were measured
      according to a rating scale. No
      significant differences in penile volume
      were noted between the rapists and the
      men convicted of non-sex crimes. The
      study did show that in rating the
      pornographic stimuli, the offenders
      convicted of non-sexual offenses evaluated
      the stimuli more positively than did the
      sexual offenders. The authors suggest that
      the pornographic stimuli was unpleasant
      for the sex offenders.

172. Kirk, Stuart A. "The Sex Offenses of Blacks and
          Whites." ARCHIVES OF SEXUAL BEHAVIOR,
          4(3): 295-302, May 1975.

          Kirk presents the results of a comparative
          study of the sex offenses of black and
          white offenders. Offender characteristics,
          types of offenses committed, and the
          characteristics of the victims were
          examined. Occupational prestige and
          social class rather than race were found
          to be the basis for the differences in
          the offenses committed by each group.
          The author concludes by discussing some
          of the dangers involved in interpreting
          the data from his study.

173. Klemmack, Susan H. and David L. Klemmack.
          "The Social Definition of Rape." in:
          Walker, Marcia J. and Stanley L. Brodsky,
          editors, SEXUAL ASSAULT. Lexington,
          Massachusetts: Lexington Books, 1976,
          pp. 135-147.

          The authors explore the legal and social
          definitions of rape in an effort to
          discover a congruency, or the absence
          of a congruency, between the definitions.
          Through the use of questionaires and
          interviews, women's social definitions
          of rape situations were gathered.
          The authors found that women's social
          definitions of rape were generally
          inconsistent with legal definitions, and
          that definitions of rape situations often
          reflected male attitudes, definitions
          of male and female sex role stereotypes,
          and prevailing myths concerning rape.

174. Koenig, Rhoda. "Rape: Most Rapidly Increasing
          Crime." MC CALLS, 100(10): 25, June 1973.

          In response to a rapid increase in rapes,
          women have established rape crisis centers
          all over the country. Koenig discusses
          the operation of some of these rape
          crisis centers, and suggests methods for
          protecting one's self against rape.

175.   Kole, Janet. "Rape and What to do About It."
        HARPER'S BAZAAR, 109(3172): 118-119,
        March 1976.

        Rape is frequently assumed to be a sexual
        crime when, in reality, it is a violent
        crime which is rooted in hostility or
        misogyny. The act of rape is a humiliation
        in which the victim is made to feel
        guilty. Kole discusses rape from a feminist
        perspective, emphasizing the sociological
        and legal aspects of the crime. The rape
        itself, and the social and legal problems
        which follow,may leave grave psychological
        scars on the victim. The operation of
        rape crisis centers to help ease the
        victim's social and psychological adjustment
        following the crime are explored. Kole
        outlines basic methods for self-protection
        against rape, and presents procedures to
        to be followed in the event that a sexual
        assault does occur. Special services
        provided for rape victims by some police
        departments are also discussed.

176.   Kollias, Karen and others.   "Women and Rape."
        MEDICAL ASPECTS OF HUMAN SEXUALITY,
        8(5): 183-197, May 1974.

        The organization and operation of the
        Washington, D.C. rape crisis center, and
        the workings of the New York City Police
        Department's Rape Squad, are the subjects
        of this interview conducted by Lorna
        Flynn. Karen Kollis, co-founder of the
        rape crisis center in Washington, D.C.,
        discusses the medical, legal, and
        psychological aspects of rape, and relates
        the methods used by the rape crisis center
        in dealing with them. Advice for dealing
        with victims of rape is also given. Julia
        Tucker, a police lieutenant and former
        head of the New York City Rape Squad,
        discusses the organization and operation
        of the squad and the evidence necessary
        for a successful rape prosecution. Tucker
        also discusses where the majority of
        rapes take place, what a victim can do
        when attacked by a rapist, and practical
        ways to prevent rape.

177. Korengold, M.C. "Victims of Rape." MEDICAL
        ANNALS OF THE DISTRICT OF COLUMBIA,
        40: 384, 1971.

    The author states that procedures for
    examining a rape victim at D.C. General
    Hospital are often delayed, or otherwise
    interrupted, thus causing additional
    emotional trauma for the victim. He
    recommends that all hospital personnel
    make a concerted effort to improve
    current methods for treating rape victims.

178. Kozol, Harry L. "Myths About the Sex Offender,"
        MEDICAL ASPECTS OF HUMAN SEXUALITY,
        5(6): 51-62, June 1971.

    Some prevalent myths about sex offenders
    are refuted in this article. Myths
    concerning homosexual as well as
    heterosexual sex offenses are discussed.
    The author feels that these myths affect
    the disposition of sex offense cases by
    the courts. Kozol states that only a
    small portion of sex offenders are
    extremely dangerous to society and it
    is this small proportion of offenders
    who should be incarcerated until their
    dangerousness has been minimized or
    eradicated.

179. Lacks, Roslyn. "The Politics of Rape--A
        Selective History." THE VILLAGE VOICE, 16
        (5):1, 44-46, February 1971.

    The author states that rape is a medium
    for expressing anger through sex, and
    that rape is an act of violence. Victims
    of rape relate their experiences,
    emphasizing the political elements of
    each particular assault. One victim,
    who had been raped twice, describes
    rape as "one of the original political
    acts--the purest form of materialism in
    an imperialist society." Lacks also
    describes other, subtler forms of rape,
    such as psychological and emotional rape,
    which leave no visible scars upon the
    victims.

180.   Lake, Alice.   "Rape: The Unmentionable Crime."
       GOOD HOUSEKEEPING, pp. 104-105,
       November 1971.

       The aftermath of a rape is frequently more
       traumatic for the victim than is the crime
       itself.   Rape victims often find that the
       responsibility for the crime is placed
       on them instead of on their assailants.
       In this selection, several rape victims
       relate their experiences with the crime.
       Lake states that the myths concerning
       rape tend to hide the facts, leaving the
       crime and its victims grossly misunderstood.
       In addition to the importance of prompt,
       thorough medical treatment by sympathetic
       hospital personnel, a sympathetic attitude
       on the part of the police is essential to
       easing the trauma experienced by rape
       victims immediately following the assault.
       The issue of balancing the rights of all
       persons involved in a crime of rape--the
       victim, the offender, and the state--is
       also discissed.   Lake concludes by suggesting
       methods for preventing rape and deterring
       a potential rapist.

181.   Lamborn, LeRoy L.   "Compensation for the Child
       Conceived in Rape."   VICTIMOLOGY: AN
       INTERNATIONAL JOURNAL, 1(1): 84-97,
       Spring 1976.

       Lamborn focuses on the special needs of a
       child conceived as a result of a rape, and
       the adequacy of methods of compensation
       available to the child.   Recognizing the
       inadequacy of traditional programs for
       compensating crime victims, New Zealand
       established an innovative compensation
       program in 1963.   This program, and
       similar programs established for the same
       purpose, provide financial assistance to
       to the victim directly injured by the
       crime, and to the dependents of deceased
       victims.   The restrictions and limitations
       of particular crime victim compensation
       programs are discussed in detail.   Lamborn
       also explores elements of the programs
       which limit the amount of benefits,

indirectly exclude the child conceived in rape from receiving benefits, deny benefits because of victim responsibility, or deny benefits on the basis of a victim-offender relationship. The author concludes by stating that although the government has the right to place restrictions on the awarding of compensation benefits to crime victims, the effect of excluding an entire class of victims from these benefits should be considered in establishing eligibility standards for compensation programs.

182. Landau, Sybil. "Rape: The Victim as Defendant." TRIAL MAGAZINE, pp. 19-22, July/August 1974.

The rising rate of rape accompanied by extremely low reporting and conviction statistics has attracted the attention of the legal system. The author discusses this phenomenon by focusing her attention on the laws and the legal system, citing apparent contradictions in them. The law appears to fail in its apparent recognition of the variety of circumstances in which a rape can occur, and treats victims as the culpable parties. Landau discusses rape and the statutory definition of rape in New York State. The New York State law incorporates stringent standards for determining the degree of resistance that a rape victim must exert in order for her participation to be rendered non-consensual by the courts. However, the courts tend to rely on their own subjective opinions concerning what constitutes the crime of rape, and these opinions and expectations may influence judicial decisions. The resistance standard in rape legislation is examined in detail, focusing on the use of actual or implied force by the assailant to demand submission from his victim. The author advocates dividing the crime of rape into degrees which reflect the amount of force employed in each particular situation. In addition, Landau states that the focus in rape cases must be shifted from the conduct of the victim to the intentions of the assailant if rape legislation is to be effective.

183. Lanham, David. "The Dangerous Sex Offender."
     MEDICAL ANNALS OF THE DISTRICT OF COLUMBIA,
     43(2): 6-7, February 1974.

     Lanham feels that the safety of the
     community at large is not given enough
     consideration when the legal system deals
     with sex offenders. The civil rights of
     the dangerous sex offender are frequently
     balanced against the safety of the
     community at large, and no genuine effort
     is made to treat or rehabilitate the
     offender. Consequently, the dangerous
     sex offender may be released from a
     correctional facility when he is not
     psychologically ready to be reintegrated
     into the community. It is suggested
     that a better understanding of the sex
     offender, his offenses, and the issues
     involved in his treatment and
     rehabilitation is needed if treatment
     and reintegration programs are to be
     effective.

184. Lanza, Charlene. "Nursing Support for the
     Victim of Sexual Assault." QUARTERLY
     REVIEW OF THE DISTRICT OF COLUMBIA
     NURSING ASSOCIATION, 39(2): 9-10,
     Summer 1971.

     In treating a sexual assault victim, the
     responsibilities of the nurse go beyond
     treating the victim's physical injuries.
     The victim's emotional and psychological
     response may have a far greater impact
     on her than the physical injuries
     sustained during the assault. Procedures
     followed by the sex crimes section of
     the police department with which the author
     works are outlined. Lanza stresses the
     importance of the attitudes displayed
     by people involved with the victim in
     aiding her emotional adjustment
     following the assault.

185. Largen, Mary Ann. "History of Women's Movement in Changing Attitudes, Laws, and Treatment Toward Rape Victims." in: Walker, Marcia J. and Stanley L. Brodsky, editors, SEXUAL ASSAULT. Lexington, Massachusetts: Lexington Books, 1976, pp. 69-73.

The influence of the women's movement in affecting change in the area of rape began in the early 1970s. Rape crisis centers were formed to counsel victims and to assist them in adjusting to their lives following the assault. Projects were initiated to bring about reform in rape laws and procedures for the treatment of rape victims by medical and law enforcement personnel. The authors note the importance of changing societal attitudes toward the problem of rape through public education programs and specialized training.

186. Lear, Martha Weinman. "Q. If You Rape a Woman and Steal Her T.V., What Can They Get You For in New York? A. Stealing Her T.V." NEW YORK TIMES MAGAZINE, p. 11, January 30, 1972.

New York State law requires that all elements of a rape be corroborated by evidence in addition to the testimony of the victim. In most other states, there is no such stringent a requirement, although some states may require a form of corroborating evidence to prove one or another of the elements necessary for an assault to be classified as a rape. The author focuses on the New York law, emphasizing the difficulty of bringing a rapist to trial and convicting him on the rape charge. In the event that a property crime is committed in conjunction with the rape, the offender will most likely be brought to trial on the robbery charge, since robbery is easier to prove, and the actual rape may be uncorroborated. Lear states that this action demonstrates the importance placed upon the protection of property. Feminists have been vocal in their opposition to New York State's "two-witness rule" for corroboration,

91

and advocate its repeal. Lear also interprets
the findings of a study conducted by Menachem
Amir, a sociologist who studied rape in
Philadelphia, Pennsylvania, and presents
the demographic patterns which had emerged
as a result of this study. In addition,
the psychology of the rapist is also
discussed, drawing on information supplied
by the Rahway Treatment Unit for Sex Offenders
in Rahway, New Jersey.

187. Lear, Martha Weinman. "What Can You Say About
Laws That Tell a Man: If You Rob a Woman
You Might as Well Rape Her Too--The Rape
is Free." REDBOOK, 139(5): 83 and 158-
167, September 1972.

Rape is a rather unusual crime: It is the
fastest rising, and yet the least understood,
of all crimes. For many, rape is repulsive,
yet attractive, embodying many of the
sexual fantasies of both man and women.
For these reasons, it is difficult to prove
rape in a court of law without outward signs
of physical abuse, such as bruises or broken
bones. Thus, the majority of rape victims
choose not to report the crimes. The laws
governing rape in New York State are
discussed as examples of laws which do
not encourage victims of rape to prosecute
their assailants. The stringent corroboration
requirements contained in the New York State
law are compared with similar requirements
applicable in other states. In addition,
societal attitudes toward rape and rape
victims are explored, emphasizing the
perpetuation of certain myths concerning
the crime. The psychology of rapists is
also discussed. Lear implies that most
women have a great fear of rape. They
fear rape, not because it is a sexual
act, but because it is a violent act of
"intimate intrusion" and violation upon
one's person, and the humiliation which
results from such an action makes the act
of rape an "unspeakable insult."

188. "The Least Punished Crime." NEWSWEEK, 80: 33,
    December 18, 1972.

    This brief comment on a Washington, D.C.
    rape and sodomy case corroborates the
    controversial image of the rape victim as
    the actual defendant during a rape trial.
    Corroboration requirements and resistance
    standards are among the issues discussed.

189. Lee, Betty. "Precautions Against Rape."
    SEXUAL BEHAVIOR, 2: 33, January 1972.

    Lee suggests procedures for women to
    follow to help prevent rape. In
    addition, to physical measures of self-
    defense, the author proposes methods
    for securing one's home and car against
    intrusion. The places where a rape is
    most likely to occur, as well as the
    conditions most conducive to sexual
    assaults, are also discussed.

190. Leggett, Stephen. "The Character of Complainants
    in Sexual Charges." CHITTY'S LAW JOURNAL,
    21: 132-135, April 1973.

    In a cross-examination as to the character
    of the complainant in a rape case, two
    extremes may be easily identified: cross-
    examination pertaining to the complainant's
    character will be completely prohibited,
    or the victim's entire prior sexual history
    will come under scrutiny by the court.
    The Canadian courts have attempted to
    establish precedents, through a series of
    significant court decisions, which avoid
    both extremes. Leggett discusses these
    decisions and summarizes the guidelines
    established for cross-examination
    concerning the complainant's general
    character and prior sexual history.

191. LeGrand, Camille. "Rape and Rape Laws: Sexism
      in Society and Law." CALIFORNIA LAW REVIEW,
      61: 919-941, May 1973.

      The threat of rape has an enormous impact
      on a woman's life. Thus, the laws governing
      the crime also affect the way in which a
      woman is forced to live her life. LeGrand
      argues that rape laws are, for the most
      part, based on traditional attitudes
      concerning the social and sexual roles of
      men and women. Instead of protecting
      women, these laws may, in fact, harm them
      by reinforcing traditional societal attitudes.
      This selection focuses on laws governing
      forcible rape. The topics discusses include:
      the extent of rape in this country, the
      characteristics of rapists and victims,
      victim-offender relationships, the
      investigation and prosecution of rape cases,
      and factors hindering rape convictions.
      The author also discusses the use of
      psychiatric examinations to reinforce the
      credibility of the complainant and to
      identify false accusations of rape. The
      consent standard in rape laws and the
      sentencing of convicted rapists are also
      explored. Possible reforms for present
      rape laws are suggested, including a
      reevaluation of punishment for the crime,
      and an improved definition of what actually
      constitutes a rape. LeGrand advocates
      reforms in the laws governing rape which
      would bring the crime into its proper
      perspective and deal with its realities.

192. Lewis, Melvin and Philip M. Sarrel. "Some
      Psychological Aspects of Seduction, Incest,
      and Rape in Childhood." JOURNAL OF THE
      AMERICAN ACADEMY OF CHILD PSYCHIATRY,
      8: 606-619, October 1969.

      The data upon which this article is based
      are drawn from cases seen or treated at a
      child psychiatric clinic and treatment
      center. The authors discuss the various
      forms of sexual assault and the possible
      psychological effects of the assault upon
      the child victim. Case studies are

employed to illustrate the impact of sexual
assault upon a child at various stages in
the child's development, and cases of
homosexual as well as heterosexual assaults
are reviewed. Lewis ans Sarrel state that
there are many factors which may influence
the child's adjustment following a sexual
assault, and that character disorder is
likely to occur if the child's psychological
trauma is not adequately and completely
overcome.

193. Libai, David. "The Protection of the Child
Victim of a Sexual Offense in the Criminal
Justice System." WAYNE LAW REVIEW, 15(2):
977-1032, Spring 1969.

Libai feels that the child victim of a
sexual offense is neglected by the legal
system. The child's psychological
condition immediately following a sexual
assault may be further damaged if the
victim is not given special consideration.
The victim's well-being may also be
endangered by lengthly or harsh interrogations
in the courtroom. The protections guarenteed
to the victim by the Constitution, and the
procedures directed at protecting the child
victim during the legal processes involved
in a sexual assault case, are among the
issues discussed.

194. Lichtenstein, Grace. "Rape Squad." NEW YORK
TIMES MAGAZINE, pp. 10-13, March 3, 1974.

The Sex Crimes Squad of the New York City
Police Department is headed by a woman
police lieutenant and staffed with female
investigators. The development of the
squad, and the controversy surrounding it,
are discussed. Its operation is explained
in detail, and some specific cases which
had been investigated by the unit are cited.

195. Lindsey, Karen and others. "Aspects of Rape."
THE SECOND WAVE: A MAGAZINE OF THE NEW
FEMINISM, 2(2): 28-29, 1972.

The authors discuss rape from a feminist
perspective. Rape is seen, both symbolically
and actually, as a tool for keeping woman
in the place created for her by the male
dominated society. In committing an act
of rape, the assailant is symbolically
violating another man's property in
addition to violating the victim's body.
Viewed from this perspective, the
psychological trauma, pain, and humiliation
suffered by the victim is ignored, and her
worth as a man's property is devalued.
It is implied that as long as our present
system of sex role socialization exists
and the myths of rape are perpetuated,
rape will continue.

196. Lipton, G.L. and E.I. Roth. "Rape: A Complex
Management Problem in the Pediatric
Emergency Room." THE JOURNAL OF PEDIATRICS,
75(5): 859-866, November 1969.

Physicians often find it difficult to
adequately diagnose injuries and propose
treatment for the child victim of rape,
due to difficulties presented by the
victim's parents, the hospital, the police,
and the victim herself. In an effort to
provide better care for the child victim,
the authors, both physicians, formulated
a plan for the management of the victim
which would allow for the study of any
complications encountered during their
treatment procedure. As a result of their
study, Lipton and Roth were able to
ascertain the nature of the problems
presented by the victim and by others
who deal with her immediately following
the assault. Recommendations are made
to remedy some of these problems and
to provide more than adequate care for
the child victim.

197. Ludwig, Frederick J. "The Case for Repeal of
the Sex Corroboration Requirement in New
York." BROOKLYN LAW REVIEW, 36(3): 378-
386, Spring 1970.

Section 130.15 of the New York State Penal
Code requires the corroboration of charges
in sex offense cases. Prior to the
enactment of this section of the penal law,
the only sex offense with a statutory
requirement of corroboration was rape
itself. Corroboration is discussed as an
obstacle to prosecution. The author presents
a case for the repeal of the corroboration
requirement, stating that the corroboration
requirement adds an additional burden of
proof to the standards required by law
for all crimes. Examples of corroboration
required in other offenses, such as
prostitution and perjury, are explored.
These corroboration requirements are
necessary only to prove that the offense
in question had actually been committed.
Ludwig states that in respect to sexual
offenses, there is no rational basis for the
inherent incredibility of the victim's
testimony. Also, the class A felonies,
which carry more severe penalties than does
rape, require no corroboration. Amendment
of the requirement as an alternative to
repeal is suggested, discussed, and rejected
by the author, who suggests that repeal is
the only fair and unequivocal solution to
the problems of corroboration.

198. Lynch, W. Ware. RAPE! ONE VICTIM'S STORY--
A DOCUMENTARY. Chicago: Follett Publishing
Company, 1974. 230 pages.

This book is based on the facts of five
actual rape cases originating in the New
York Criminal Courts. Lynch begins his
narrative with the commission of the rape
and ends it with the jury verdict following
the trial. The victim's psychological
reaction to the rape is portrayed, and
the medical and legal processes involved
in the investigation of a rape case are
discussed.

199. McCaldron, R.J. "Rape." CANADIAN JOURNAL OF
     CORRECTIONS, 9: 37-58, 1967.

    McCaldron reviews the history of rape and
rape laws, emphasizing the punishments
prescribed for the crime during various
periods in history. Sections of the Canadian
Criminal Code which are concerned with rape
are also examined. Because of the
seriousness of rape and the severity of
sentences for the crime, in addition to
the scarcity of significant literature on
the subject, research was initiated in which
thirty convicted rapists serving sentences
for the crime were studied. Demographic
variables are presented and psychological
issues are discussed. The factors examined
in this study include: the nature and
location of the offense, association of
alcohol with the offense, health and employment
records of the offenders, prior criminal
records, psychological diagnosis of the
offender, the length of sentence, adjustment
of the offender to life in prison, and the
potential for psychiatric treatment of
rapists and paedophiles. The author also
classified the rapists studied into three
general catagories: the unlucky offender
who repeatedly rapes but is never convicted;
the sociopathic rapist who is characterized
as antisocial, egocentric, and devoid of
meaningful relationships with others; the
defensive rapists, who rape out of fear or
hostility toward women. McCaldron concludes
this selection by discussing the potential
of these offenders for psychiatric treatment.

200. McCarthy, Colman. "The Crime of Rape." THE
     WASHINGTON POST, August 8, 1973.

    The psychological effect of rape upon the
victim is discussed in detail. The author
states that rape is a psychological as well
as a physical violation, and that the crime
may cause serious damage to the victim's
emotional and psychological health. Referring
to the work of Dr. John M. Macdonald, McCarthy
describes three phases which occur in the
psychological adjustment of the victim
following a sexual assault. This article

concludes with statements concerning
the difficulty of changing societal
attitudes toward the crime of rape and
the rape victim.

201. McCombie, Sharon and others. "Development of a
Medical Center Rape Crisis Intervention
Program." AMERICAN JOURNAL OF PSYCHIATRY,
133(4): 418-421, April 1976.

In order to provide psychiatric counseling
for victims of sexual assault, a rape
crisis intervention program was developed
at a large, metropolitan teaching hospital
in Boston, Massachusetts. The program
was developed on the assumption that
early treatment can prevent the development
of psychological problems which may result
from a sexual assault. The authors discuss
the need for such a crisis intervention
program, and outline some of the policy,
financial, and personnel problems encountered
in establishing the program. The operation
of the program is described in detail, and
its importance as a community resource
center is noted.

202. McCubbin, and Scott. "Management of Alleged
Sexual Assault." TEXAS MEDICINE, 69:
59-64, September 1973.

The medical examination and collection of
physical evidence in alleged rape cases
are discussed in detail. Methods of medical
treatment for victims of sexual assaults
are presented, and follow-up procedures,
including medical and counseling programs,
are outlined.

203. McDermott, Thomas E. "California Rape Evidence
Reform: An Analysis of Senate Bill 1678."
THE HASTINGS LAW JOURNAL, 26(6): 1551-1573,
May 1975.

Before beginning his discussion of California's
Evidence Code and Senate Bill 1678, McDermott
relates the details of a 1955 rape case, in
which the victim's prior sexual conduct was

admitted into evidence during the trial. It is this issue and the controversy surrounding it that led the California Legislature to enact a series of laws and resolutions to protect the rights of rape victims. One such bill is Senate Bill 1678, which makes a victim's prior sexual conduct generally inadmissible as evidence in a rape case. Problems associated with prosecutions of rape cases, and the California Evidence Code itself are discussed, focusing on the intended effect of Senate Bill 1678. Following detailed discussions of issues related to evidence and Senate Bill 1678, the author concludes that the bill is not effective in reforming the California Evidence Code, and in encouraging more women to report and prosecute the crime. Recommendations for further reforms are also suggested.

204. MacDonald, John M. RAPE OFFENDERS AND THEIR VICTIMS. Springfield, Illinois: Charles C. Thomas, Publisher, 1971. 342 pages.

In this very detailed work, the author explores many facets of rape. The first chapter, entitled, "The Scope of Rape," discusses the extent of rape by presenting a variety of rape cases and situations as examples. Types of rapes presented in this section include: group rapes, sadistic rapes, and the rape of children. The second chapter defines forcible rape and explores the incidence of rape by discussing rape rates in the United States and in other countries, the place of the initial meeting between offender and victim, and the location and time of the offense. MacDonald devotes the rest of this book to the following topics: victim and offender characteristics, the rape of children, group rape, the psychology of rape, rape and homicide, incest, rape and the law, rape prevention, treatment and punishment, and false accusations of rape.

This book also includes a six-page general bibliography on rape.

205. McDormich, Shirley. "Popular Myths About Rape."
      STRAIGHT CREEK JOURNAL, pp. 8-9,
      August 28-September 4, 1973.

      The misunderstandings concerning rape may
      be attributed, in part, to the abundance
      of myths justifying the crime. The
      author discusses many of these myths in
      detail, emphasizing the effect of sex-role
      socialization in the perpetuation of myths
      concerning rape. Some popular rape myths
      include: every woman secretly wants to be
      raped, the victims of rape are all sexually
      aggressive women, rape is woman's favorite
      sexual fantasy, most rape victims make
      false rape reports and had not been raped
      at all, society will usually sympathize
      with the rape victim, the man is not
      responsible for the crime, police do not
      believe a woman placing a rape complaint.
      McDormich explains why these myths are
      usually not supported by facts. Methods
      for deterring a potential rapist and
      possibly preventing the crime are also
      suggested.

206. McDowell, Joseph F. "Constitutional Law--
      Cruel and Unusual Punishment." SUFFOLK
      LAW REVIEW, 5(2): 504-512, Winter 1971.

      The focus of this selection is the rape
      case of Ralph v. Warden, 438 F.2d 786
      (4th cir, 1970), a 1970 case originating
      in Maryland. Ralph had been found guilty
      of rape and had been sentenced to death
      pursuant to Maryland law. The Court
      of Appeals reversed the decision, saying
      that it constituted cruel and unusual
      punishment as prohibited by the eighth
      amendment to the United States Constitution,
      since the victim's life was not taken nor
      endangered. This decision is discussed
      in light of other decisions concerning
      similar issues of constitutionality.
      McDowell concludes with the hope that
      capital punishment in general will be
      eliminated, or at least eliminated in
      cases where it is disproportional to the
      crime committed.

207. McGillicuddy, Michael. "Criminal Law: Mistake of Age as Defense to Statutory Rape." UNIVERSITY OF FLORIDA LAW REVIEW, 18: 699-703, Spring 1966.

Most courts in the United States have held that a reasonable mistake of age in cases of statutory rape is not a valid defense for the crime. In the case of People v. Hernandez, 61 Cal.2d 529, 393 P.2d 673, 39 Cal Rptr. 361 (1964), the California Supreme Court ruled that the defendant's reasonable mistake of age in this statutory rape case could be used as a defense. McGillicuddy discusses the Florida statutory rape statute, which does not allow mistake of age as a defense for statutory rape. The existence of varying degrees of responsibility in statutory rape cases is acknowledged, as is the need to protect young children from sexual abuse by adults. In light of these facts, the author recommends that a reasonable mistake of age be admissible as a defense in statutory rape cases in Florida.

208. MacInnes, Colin. "One Reading of Rape." NEW SOCIETY, 33(667): 147, July 17, 1975.

Some prevalent attitudes toward rape are presented in an attempt to explain the crime. The author divides rape into various catagories: military rapes, political rapes, neurotic rapes, and rapes which occur because a man misinterprets "the sexual courting signals." Each catagory is described in detail, and examples are provided. MacInnes also discusses typical male and female attitudes toward rape, and suggests methods to be employed by women as potential victims, and men as possible assailants, for preventing rapes.

209. MacKellar, Jean. RAPE: THE BAIT AND THE TRAP. New York: Crown Publishers, 1975. 154 pages.

MacKellar provides a sympathetic analysis of rape by exploding myths and raising some controversal questions. Victim and offender

characteristics, locations most conducive
to attack, gang rape, rape and the legal
system, and methods of prevention are
among the topics discussed. In attempting
to find probable causes for rape, sociological
and psychological factors affecting the crime
are explored. The author feels that rape is
rooted in cultural attitudes toward the roles
of males and females in society and that,
until these attitudes are changed, it will
be difficult to find an effective solution
to the problem.

210. MacNamara, Donal E.J. and Milton Helpern.
"Sexual Crimes and the Medical Examiner."
MEDICAL ASPECTS OF HUMAN SEXUALITY, 8(4):
161-168, April 1974.

Helpern states that there is a definite
correlation between sex and violent crime,
and that a significant number of homicides
in New York are associated with sexual
assault. Physical evidence needed to
discover the identity of a sexual offender
is discussed in detail. Homosexual
homicides, and homicides steming from other
types of deviant sexual behavior,are also
discussed through the use of examples from
actual cases. Regarding homicide between
married people, marital violence based on
infidelity,or suspected infidelity,is
explored. The selection ends with a
commentary which presents, in detail, the
evidence collected in various types of sexual
assault-homicides.

211. MacNamara, Donal E.J. and John J. Sullivan.
"Making the Victim Whole." THE URBAN REVIEW,
6(3): 21-25, 1973.

Monetary compensation to victims of crime
is the subject of this article. The authors
explain contemporary crime victim
compensation statutes and compare them
with methods of restitution and compensation
throughout history. The criteria for
granting compensation are explored with the
aid of accounts from actual cases where
compensation was either granted or withheld.

It is the opinion of the authors that crime
victim compensation is necessary and that
victim compensation statutes should be
retained, or initiated if they do not
already exist in a juristiction.

212. Maloney, Sharon. "Rape in Illinois: A Denial
of Equal Protection." THE JOHN MARSHALL
JOURNAL OF PRACTICE AND PROCEDURE,
8: 457-496, Spring 1975.

The Illinois Criminal Code governing sexual
offenses classifies forcible, vaginal sexual
intercourse as rape, and forcible anal or
oral intercourse as deviate sexual assault.
In making this distinction, the courts tend
to treat women, who are victims of rape as
defined by this statute, quite differently
than men or women who are victims of an
act defined as a deviate sexual assault.
The rules of evidence for rape cases tend
to be more stringent than those for other
sexual offenses. Maloney implies that
because of this apparent segregation in
the law of forcible sexual assault on the
basis of "the anatomical difference between
men and women," women are denied equal
protection under this law. In exploring this
issue, the author discusses the issue of
consent, the development of the definitions
of deviate sexual assault and rape, evidence
employed to impeach the credibility of the
complainant in a rape case and in a case of
deviate sexual assault, and chastity of
the rape victim. The issues of credibility,
chastity, and resistance in rape cases are
compared with similar issues in cases of
deviate sexual assault. Concerning equal
protection under the law, as guarenteed by
the Illinois Constitution, the author
explores various tests frequently employed
to determine if equal protection has been
denied. She concludes that in order to
establish equal protection for all victims
of sexual aggression, rules governing the
admissibility of evidence to prove force
must be uniformly applied to all sexually
aggressive acts.

213. Manville, W.H. "Mind of the Rapist." COSMOPOLITAN,
176(1): 74-77, January 1974.

The psychology of rapists is discussed with
the aid of case studies. The psychoanalyst
quoted in this article states that a rapist's
initial aggressive action in a sexual
situation is not transformed into a sensual
response, as in "normal" men. Rather, the
rapist's "aggressive drive" becomes distorted
and is channeled into destructive aggressive
behavior. This psychoanalyst also suggests
that it is possible for a potential rape
victim to prevent rape from occurring,
and recommends methods which may be effective
in doing so.

214. Margolin, Deborah. "Rape: The Facts." WOMEN:
A JOURNAL OF LIBERATION, 3(1): 19-22, 1972.

The author presents statistics as evidence
of the high incidence of rape. Statistics
are also provided which discuss the locations
of sexual assaults, victim characteristics,
and the number of rapes reported to law
enforcement personnel. Differential legal
treatment on the basis of race is mentioned,
and concern for the problem of falsely
reporting a rape, and the effects of such
an action on the legal system, is discussed.
The medical examination of the rape
victim is critically examined, as is the
court procedure followed during a rape
trial. Margolin concludes with a brief
discussion of support services organized
by women and women's groups to assist
rape victims.

215. Markillie, Ronald E.D. "Sex Offenders in Prison."
in: Slovenko, Ralph, editor, SEXUAL
BEHAVIOR AND THE LAW. Springfield,
Illinois: Charles C. Thomas, Publisher,
1965, pp. 779-804.

Markillie studied offenders convicted of
sexual crimes and sentenced to prison terms.
Problems encountered by the psychotherapist
in attempting to treat the sex offender
in prison are discussed, and the value of
the treatment received by an offender in

a prison setting is questioned. The offenders'
motives for committing sexual offenses and
their reasons for seeking treatment are
explored. The author suggests that many sex
offenders encounter difficulties in adjusting
to life in prison and that treatment programs
should be more positive by directing
treatment toward the offender's eventual
return to the community.

216. Massey, J.B. and others. "Management of Sexually
      Assaulted Females." OBSTETRICS AND GYNECOLOGY,
      38(1): 29-36, July 1971.

      The program for treatment of sexual assault
      victims examined at Philadelphia General
      Hospital in Philadelphia, Pennsylvania is
      described in detail. The medicolegal
      examination of a sexual assault victim is
      viewed as a major responsibility of the
      attending physician, and is discussed in
      relation to evidence necessary for
      corroborating a charge of rape. Methods
      for preventing venereal disease, pregnancy,
      and psychological damage to the victim are
      also described. In discussing the child
      victim of a sexual offense, the authors
      state that children are not "mentally
      asexual," and usually willingly participate
      in the act.

217. Masters, William H. and Virginia E. Johnson.
      "The Aftermath of Rape." REDBOOK MAGAZINE,
      147(2): 74-161, June 1976.

      The psychological and physiological effects
      of rape on the victim are discussed. The
      authors suggest that, in general, not
      enough attention is given to the psychological
      trauma suffered by the sexual assault victim
      immediately following the attack, or to the
      possibility of psychological damage occurring
      in the future. Some particular forms of
      physical and psychological trauma are
      explored, including the most frequent problems
      experienced by sexually traumatized women.
      Masters and Johnson also discuss the response
      of a victims husband to the rape, and the
      psychology of the rapist. This article

concludes by attributing the compulsion to rape to the concept of woman as a "sexual servant" rather than as an equal partner in a sexual experience.

218. Mathiasen, Sally. "The Rape Victim: A Victim of Society and Law." WILLAMETTE LAW JOURNAL 11(1): 36-55, Winter 1974.

Rape is defined according to the statutory laws of Washington and Oregon. The author states that the rules governing the admissibility of evidence in a rape trial protect the defendant at the expense of the victim. Since a rape is usually not directly observed, the only witnesses to the crime are the victim and the defendant. During the trial, the question of culpability focuses on whether the jury finds the testimony of the victim, or of the defendant, more credible. The defense attorney will attempt to introduce evidence which will discredit the testimony of the victim. This process often involves questions dealing with the victim's general character and reputation in an attempt to impeach her credibility, or to prove that she consented to sexual intercourse with the defendant. Mathiasen discusses the law as it is written and as it is practiced by the police, the prosecutor, the defense attorney, the judge, and the jury. Many states have initiated legislation in an attempt to reform existing rape laws. Some suggestions for legislative reform are presented, emphasizing the need for reform in the area of the admissibility of evidence concerning a victim's prior sexual activity with men other than the defendant. Mathiasen concludes by suggesting that when the rape victim is no longer subject to the biases of the legal system, which is based on outdated moral and social attitudes toward sex roles, the victim, and not the defendant, will receive the support of the courts during the trial process.

219.   Medea, Andra and Kathleen Thompson. AGAINST RAPE.
        New York: Farrar, Straus, and Giroux, 1974.
        152 pages.

        AGAINST RAPE may be termed a kind of textbook
        on rape for women. Medea and Thompson discuss
        everything from the possible causes of rape
        to movements for preventing it. The
        sociological and psychological bases for
        rape, legal procedures followed in rape
        cases, verbally abusive behavior toward
        women (termed "the little rapes" by the
        authors), and the development of organizations
        against rape are among the topics discussed.
        An illustrated section on self-defense, a
        general bibliography, and a listing of rape
        crisis centers around the country are included.

220.   Medea, Andra and Kathleen Thompson. "How Much
        Do You Really Know About Rapists?" MS.
        MAGAZINE, 3(1): 113-114, July 1974.

        Any woman is a potential rape victim. A
        women's movements and activities must be
        conducted according to established rules
        formulated by the male dominated society.
        If a woman violates these rules, she is
        fair game for the rapist, and the chances
        of her assailant being convicted for the
        crime are very slim. To illustrate these
        points, and to correct some misconceptions
        concerning rape, the authors present some
        typical accounts of sexual assault. "An
        exaggerated image of masculinity" and the
        desire for sexual gratification are
        identified as motivations behind the
        commission of a rape. The authors conclude
        by stating that many so-called "ordinary
        men" who fail to view women as human
        beings may, indeed, be potential rapists.

221.   Mehrhof, Barbara and Pamela Kearon. "Rape: An
        Act of Terror." in: NOTES FROM THE THIRD
        YEAR, New York: Women's Liberation Press,
        1972, pp. 79-81.

        Rape is viewed as the product of a male
        dominated society. The female is subservient
        to the male, and the relationship between

male and female is understood by the authors
as a superior/inferior relationship in which
women are equated with slaves. The authors
state that rape is a terror tactic which
women accept as an inevitable product of
male domination and the "sexist ideology."
Rape, as supported by a consensus of
 males, is a "political act of oppression."
The authors advocate the establishment of
a "counter-reality" by women, in which
the hold of male domination and the "sexist
ideology" will be destroyed.

222.   Metzger, Deena.   "It Is Always the Woman Who
        Is Raped." AMERICAN JOURNAL OF PSYCHIATRY,
        133(4): 405-408, April 1976.

        Metzger views rape as an act of aggression
        that is condoned by society through literature
        and the media. Rape strips a woman of her
        humanity, leaving a woman to define herself
        as a "nonperson." The image of rape as an
        accepted symbol of male power and domination
        is discussed. The solution to the problem
        of rape must come from women who speak out
        against their powerlessness and proclaim
        themselves as persons.

223.   Mintz, Betty.   "Patterns in Forcible Rape: A
        Review-Essay." CRIMINAL LAW BULLETIN,
        9: 703-710, October 1973.

        Menachem Amir's PATTERNS IN FORCIBLE RAPE
        has been recognized as a significant
        contribution to the scientific study of
        rape. Mintz feels that Amir's work does
        not adequately explain the sociological
        aspects of rape. Amir's conclusions
        include the existence of a subculture of
        violence responsible for rape, which is
        subject to criticism in this review. Other
        areas of disagreement between Amir and Mintz
        include: race, victim precipitation, the
        relationship between offender and victim, and
        characteristics of victims and offenders.
        Amir's methodology is also criticized for
        the weakness of the sample selected for
        study. Mintz concludes that Amir's work
        does, in fact, confuse the reader as to
        the social issues involved in the crime.

224. Musman, Jeffrey L. "Constitutional Law--Death
     Penalty as Cruel and Unusual Punishment
     for Rape." WILLIAM AND MARY LAW REVIEW,
     12(3): 682-687, Spring 1971.

     On an appeal in a Maryland case, Ralph v.
     Warden, 438 F.2d 786 (4th cir. 1970), the
     United States Court of Appeals held that
     the defendant could not be executed for
     rape because to do so would constitute
     cruel and unusual punishment as prohibited
     by the eighth amendment to the United States
     Constitution, since the victim's life was
     not endangered. In addition to the case of
     Ralph v. Warden, other cases in which the
     eighth or fourteenth amendment was an
     issue are discussed. Musman states that
     the significance of the holding in Ralph v.
     Warden lies in the fact that it was the
     first case in which the death penalty for
     rape was found to be cruel and unusual
     punishment according to the proscription
     of the eighth amendment.

225. Myers, Larry W. "Reasonable Mistake of Age:
     A Needed Defense to Statutory Rape."
     MICHIGAN LAW REVIEW, 64: 105-136,
     November 1965.

     The author recognizes the need for reform
     in the laws governing statutory rape. It
     is often difficult to judge a person's age
     by appearance, and the age at which a woman
     is deemed capable of consent to sexual
     relations must be an arbitrary determination.
     The treatment of the issue concerning a
     reasonable mistake of age on the part of the
     defendant by the American courts is compared
     with that of the European and South African
     courts. The requirement of Mens Rea is
     discussed as it applies to statutory rape
     and various other types of offenses. Offenses
     not requiring the presense of Mens Rea, such
     as public welfare offenses, are also
     mentioned. The culpability of the defendant
     and the prosecutrix in a case of statutory
     rape is also explored. Myers presents
     recommendations for reform in laws governing
     statutory rape. These recommendations include:

a reclassification of females by age, thus placing offenses into one of two distinct catagories which impose different degrees of liability; application of an age differential between males and females before strict liability for the offense could be imposed; the establishment of definite standards of culpability.

226. Nelson, Steve and Menachem Amir. "The Hitchhike Victim of Rape: A Research Report." in: Drapko, Israel and Emilio Viano, VICTIMOLOGY: A NEW FOCUS, Volume 5. Lexington, Mass.: Lexington Books, 1975, pp. 47-64.

When a woman hitchhikes, she is seen as a violator of the mores of American society, and is, therefore, responsible for whatever problems ensue from the ·hitchhiking situation. The authors reviewed rape complaints received by the Berkeley, California Police Department over a six-year period in order to ascertain whether a relationship existed between the increase in reported rapes, and hitchhiking. Racial and age patterns were studied, and the characteristics of victims and offenders were identified. A definite relationship was found between hitchhiking and the increase of reported rapes in the city of Berkeley. The authors assumed that if there had been no significant number of female hitchhikers, the rate of reported rapes would have been proportionally reduced; this was not the case.

227. Newman, Holly. "Dealing With Rape." THE SECOND WAVE: A MAGAZINE OF THE NEW FEMINISM, 3: 36-37, 1973.

Women are developing their own methods for dealing with the crime of rape. Newman discusses the establishment of rape crisis centers across the country, and the problems associated with their development and operation. Other ideas suggested for preventing rape or educating women and the public about rape include research projects, increased communication between women's groups and the public, and distribution of literature on rape.

228. Noland, William. "Other Crimes Evidence to
     Prove Intent in Rape Cases." LOYOLA LAW
     REVIEW, 19(3): 751-758, Fall 1973.

     In a rehearing of State v. Moore, 278 So.
     2d 784 (La. 1973), the Supreme Court held
     that the trial court had been in error in
     allowing the defendant's prior offenses
     to be admitted into evidence in order to
     show intent in the present case. Since
     the case involved aggravated rape, it was
     not necessary to prove intent. The
     author discusses cases which had set
     precedents in the admission of a defendant's
     prior arrest records into evidence in order
     to prove intent in rape cases. Several
     recent aggravated rape cases are also
     discussed. Noland states that if a rape
     case is brought before the court, the
     decision to admit a defendant's prior
     offence record in order to prove intent
     in the case presently before the court
     should rest on whether or not intent is an
     issue in the case. If the issue of intent
     is not relevant to the case, the admission
     of evidence to prove intent is also irrelevant
     and must be ruled inadmissible.

229. Notman, Malkah T. and Carol C. Nadelson.
     "The Rape Victim: Psychodynamic Considerations."
     AMERICAN JOURNAL OF PSYCHIATRY, 133(4): 409-
     412, April 1976.

     Women have various reactions to rape.
     Drawing upon a study conducted by Burgess
     and Holmstrom, Notman and Nadelson discuss
     the possible psychological reactions of
     victims to rape, including their methods
     for adjusting to the aftermath of the crime.
     The attitudes of psychiatrists toward the
     rape victim are also discussed. The authors
     emphasize the victim's need for support and
     reassurance in order for her to better adapt
     to her life following the assault. It is
     suggested that the counselor help provide
     this support.

230. Oestreicher, David. "Evidence--Criminal Law--
     Prior Sexual Offenses Against a Person
     Other Than the Prosecutrix." TULANE LAW
     REVIEW, 46(2): 336-343, December 1971.

     In the case of State v. Bolden, 257 La.
     60, 241 So.2d 490 (1970), evidence of a
     prior sexual offense committed against a
     person other than the complaining witness
     in the present case had been admitted into
     the trial. The defense attorney's objection
     to the admissibility of this testimony on
     the grounds that it was irrelevant to the
     present crime was overruled by the court.
     On appeal, the Louisiana Supreme Court
     affirmed the lower court's conviction
     and held that evidence of crimes similar
     to the crime for which the defendant was
     on trial was admissible to show intent in
     the present case. The author examines other
     Louisiana cases in which the admission of
     prior sexual offenses had been an issue.
     He concludes by stating that an accused
     sexual offender is more susceptible to
     injustice if his prior sexual offenses are
     brought to the attention of the jury. Each
     court, therefore, should rule on the
     admissibility of such evidence on a case
     by case basis, without the jury present.

231. Offir, Carole Wade. "Don't Take It Lying Down."
     PSYCHOLOGY TODAY, 8(8): 73, January 1975.

     Various opinions exist concerning methods
     to be employed by potential victims in
     order to prevent rape. This article suggests
     some reasonable methods which can be used
     by any woman to defend herself, while warning
     against employing methods which may do more
     harm than good. Offir stresses the
     importance, to the victim, of acting
     quickly anf following through with a
     prevention tactic, using any weapon at her
     disposal.

232. Pacht, Asher R. "The Rapist in Treatment:
      Professional Myths and Psychological
      Realities." in: Walker, Marcia J. and
      Stanley L. Brodsky, editors, SEXUAL ASSAULT.
      Lexington, Massachusetts: Lexington Books,
      1976, pp. 91-97.

      Three myths which may hinder the successful
      treatment of the convicted rapist are examined
      in detail. Pacht contradicts information
      which supports these myths by presenting
      the findings of research in addition to
      concrete examples. The need for change in
      treatment approaches is discussed. The
      author explores what he terms "typical
      efforts" for treating sex offenders,
      hightlighting promising innovative programs
      in addition to the most successful traditional
      ones. He concludes by expressing the
      necessity for controlled research programs
      in order to determine appropriate treatment
      procedures for convicted rapists.

233. Partington, Donald H. "The incidence of the Death
      Penalty for Rape in Virginia." WASHINGTON
      AND LEE LAW REVIEW, 22(1): 43-63, Spring 1965.

      Upon examination of records of the state of
      Virginia concerning the incidence of the
      death penalty for rape, one instantly
      suspects that the death penalty had been
      differentially applied. It is evident that
      a much larger proportion of blacks had
      received the death penalty for rape in
      Virginia than had whites, and since 1908,
      no white man has actually been executed.
      The factors involved in raising the issue
      of denial of equal protection in light of
      these facts include: appellate review of
      rape cases, history of punishments for rape,
      crime rates by race, executions in
      juristictions other than Virginia, and
      non-capital punishments for rape. Partington
      discusses the constitutionality of various
      statutes imposing punishment and authorizing
      sentencing by a jury, disparity of
      punishment, the unconstitutionality of the
      death penalty under the eighth amendment,
      and the issue of denial of equal protection.
      He concludes that a solution to the

sentencing problem in Virginia is for that
state to adopt a mandatory system of
appellate review for all death penalty cases.

234. Pekkanen, John. VICTIMS: AN ACCOUNT OF RAPE.
New York: Dial Press, 1976. 287 pages.

Based on an actual rape case, VICTIMS: AN
ACCOUNT OF RAPE compassionately explores
the problem of rape from the viewpoints of
the victim, a police detective, the defense
attorney, and the prosecutor. Pekkanen's
central point is that there are actually
two victims involved in a crime of rape,
and that the trauma for one is as great as
the trauma for the other. The first victim,
the actual rape victim, is traumatized not
only by her assailant but also by the criminal
justice system. Pekkanen's sympathy also
lies with the second victim, the rapist, who,
Pekkanen feels, is unjustly treated and
irreparably damaged by the criminal justice
system and social welfare institutions which
serve the rape victim.

235. Perr, Irwin N. "Statutory Rape of an Insane
Person." JOURNAL OF FORENSIC SCIENCES,
13(4): 433-441, October 1968.

The issue of consent is an important one
when discussing the crime of rape. The
author of this selection distinguishes
between the expressions "against her will"
and "without her consent," stating that
a victim may be legally unable to give
consent due to circumstances which may alter
her ability to rationally consent. Perr
discusses, in detail, a case of rape in which
the victim, a woman with a mental disability,
was legally unable to rationally give her
consent to the act.

236. Peters, Joseph J. "Child Rape: Defusing a
Psychological Time Bomb." HOSPITAL
PHYSICIAN, 8: 46-49, February 1973.

The psychological effects of rape on a female
child may have damaging consequences for her

115

psychological and psychosexual development.
The child victim tends to emotionally
withdraw from the aftermath of rape, as
opposed to the adult victim's outwardly
directed emotional response. Peters
siggests ways in which the emergency room
physician can aid in the psychological
repairing of the child victim. He feels
that if sufficient attention is given to
the victim's emotional needs following
the assault, psychosexual problems occurring
in later life as a result of the rape
experience may be minimized or eliminated.

237. Peters, Joseph J. "The Philadelphia Rape Victim
Study." in: Drapkin, Israel and Emilio
Viano, VICTIMOLOGY: A NEW FOCUS, Volume
III. Lexington, Massachusetts: Lexington
Books, 1975, pp. 181-199.

Recognizing the lack of significant literature
focusing on the victims of sexual assaults,
the Philadelphia General Hospital Center
for Rape Concern was established. The
center focuses its studies on the
psychological and social effects of rape
victimization. The establishment and
operation of this center are described in
detail, emphasizing the victim's need for
immediate treatment and follow-up care.
A sample of data collected by the center
is examined, and some conclusions and
generalizations are drawn from the analysis.
The reaction of the police to rape and the
rape victim, the problem of victim credibility,
and the effects of rape on the child victim
are also discussed.

238. Peters, Joseph J. "Social, Legal, and Psychological
Effects of Rape on the Victim." PENNSYLVANIA
MEDICINE, 78(2): 34-36, February 1975.

The credibility of the rape victim is
frequently questioned by hospital personnel,
the courts, and the police. The Philadelphia
General Hospital's Center for Rape Concern
often treats rape victims who have been
turned away from other medical facilities.

Peters discusses the reactions of the victims'
families, some police, medical, and court
personnel toward rape and the rape victim.
Evidence collected by medical personnel
during their examination of a rape victim
is mentioned, in addition to the evidentiary
requirements necessary to substantiate a
charge of rape. The psychological trauma
experienced by a rape victim is also of
concern to the author in this article. He
discusses the psychological and emotional
reactions to the rape, and identifies the
most common fears and complaints of distress
frequently demonstrated by rape victims.

239. Peters, Joseph J. and Hermann A. Roether.
      "Group Psychotherapy of Probationed Sex
      Offenders." INTERNATIONAL PSYCHIATRY
      CLINICS, 8: 69-80, 1972.

      The group psychotherapy program used by the
      clinic at Philadelphia General Hospital to
      treat probationed sex offenders is explained
      in detail. Problems associated with this
      type of treatment are explored, in addition
      to its advantages. Characteristics of the
      patients treated by the clinic in a group
      psychotherapy situation, the group process
      itself, and the necessary length of
      treatment are among the topics discussed.
      The authors state that the group process
      of psychotherapy lends needed support to
      the offender by placing him in a situation
      with people of similar backgrounds and
      problems who have committed similar offenses.
      It was discovered that the offenders spent
      a considerable amount of time discussing
      common personal and social problems, and
      giving each other support. Thus, the
      authors view group psychotherapy as a
      successful method of treatment for convicted
      sex offenders.

240. Peters, Joseph J. and Robert L. Sadoff.
      "Psychiatric Services for Sex Offenders
      on Probation." FEDERAL PROBATION, 35(3):
      33-37, September 1971.

      This article explores the possibilities of
      establishing a successful psychiatric outpatient

clinic for convicted sex offenders. The
authors begin by stating that the sex offenders
on probation are usually suffering primarily
from character or personality disorders
and that they are not usually welcomed for
treatment by most treatment agencies. The
need for group psychotherapy for the sex
offender was consequently recognized by
Peters and others. In this article, the
factors necessary for a successful group
psychotherapy clinic (the psychiatrist,
the court, the probation department, and the
offender) are discussed and solutions to
potential problems are suggested. The
authors also present what they see to be the
definite advantages of group psychotherapy
over individual psychotherapy for sex
offenders on probation. They conclude that
group psychotherapy is much more acceptable
to the offender and can be more beneficial
to his psychological well-being and
community adjustment problems than can
individual therapy.

241. Pieragostini, Dennis L. "Reasonable Mistake
as to Age--A Defense to Statutory Rape
Under the New Penal Code." CONNECTICUT
LAW REVIEW, 2(2): 433-441, Winter 1969-1970.

If the victim in a statutory rape case
appeared to be older than her actual age,
can the defendant's reasonable mistake as
to the age of the victim be used as a defense
in his trial? This is the question raised
and discussed in this article. Pieragostini
presents theories dealing with the question
of mistaken age in statutory rape cases,
and discusses already existing standards
for determining if there was, in fact, a
case of mistaken age and justifications for
the existence of it as a defense. He
concludes that such a rule is necessary
in order to absolve a defendant of criminal
liability when there was no intention on
his part to commit a crime.

242. Pilpel, Harriet F. "Sex vs. the Law." JOURNAL
      OF THE AMERICAN MEDICAL WOMEN'S ASSOCIATION,
      23(2): 179-184, February 1968.

      The author feels that America's sex laws
      are outdated and unnecessary. Citing the
      difference between the need for laws
      prohibiting violent sexual behavior and the
      need for laws prohibiting other forms of
      sexual behavior, Pilpel feels that laws
      prohibiting the former are necessary and
      laws prohibiting the latter are an
      unnecessary impingement on a person's
      privacy. Ending on a hopeful note, the
      author feels that there is a movement away
      from unnecessary laws prohibiting non-violent,
      consensual sexual behavior.

243. Pittler, Robert M. "Existentialism and Corroboration
      of Sex Crimes in New York: A New Attempt to
      Limit 'If Someone Didn't See It, It Didn't
      Happen'." SYRACUSE LAW REVIEW, 24: 1-37,
      1973.

      In 1972, the New York State Legislature
      enacted amendments to that state's corroboration
      requirements for rape cases. The new law is
      summarized, emphasizing changes in the
      requirements for corroborating evidence.
      The amended law is discussed in detail and
      comparisons are made between the law as
      amended and the prior law. In his conclusion,
      the author states that the amended law is
      the result of a compromise between those
      who desired a very stringent corroboration
      requirement--a situation which resulted in
      relatively few convictions--and those who
      wanted no corroboration requirement. Pitler
      feels that the amended law's greatest failure
      can be found in the fact that the increased
      burden of proof is placed on the prosecutor,
      who must corroborate any sexual contact,
      be it a completed, or an attempted, act.

244. Podolsky, Edward. "The Lust Murderer."
      MEDICO-LEGAL JOURNAL, 33: 174-178,
      1965.

      This article discusses the psychology of the
      murderer whose crime has definite sexual roots.

The characteristics of the typical lust
murderer are presented and various cases
are discussed. Podolsky states that many
rape-murders are committed because the
murderer fears the consequences of, and
societal reactions to, his aggressive,
violent sexual act.

245. "Police Discretion and the Judgement that a Crime
Has been Committed--Rape in Philadelphia."
UNIVERSITY OF PENNSYLVANIA LAW REVIEW,
117: 277-322, 1968.

It is a function of the police to determine
if a crime has, in fact, occurred, and to
collect information to be used in making
this determination. This selection focuses
on the discretion employed by police in
Philadelphia, Pennsylvania to determine
that a crime of rape has been committed.
The responses of police to certain variables
(for example, the promptness of reporting
of a complaint; physical condition of the
victim) were analyzed in order to ascertain
whether the procedures outlined for the
police were being followed. The police
responses are discussed in detail, as
are the procedures followed in the
investigation of a rape complaint. The
use of polygraph examinations in a rape
investigation is also explored, and
recommendations for improvements in the
police procedures for investigating rape
complaints are suggested.

246. Pollner, Fran. "Rape in the Courtroom." OFF OUR
BACKS, 3: 2-3, December 1972.

This article focuses on a Washington, D.C.
rape and sodomy case. The problems of
complainant credibility, racial stereotypes,
and the resistance standard in rape cases
are discussed. Pollner concludes by
presenting some suggested methods for
preventing rape, including illustrations of
successful self defense tactics.

247. "Portrait of a Rapist." NEWSWEEK, 82: 67-68,
     August 20, 1973.

   This selection discusses the psychology
   of rapists through the use of case studies.
   Two different motivations are suggested
   for the crime of rape, in addition to sexual
   gratification. A psychologist describes
   these motivations as aggressive feelings
   toward women and a combination of sexual
   desire and sadism. An important distinction
   made between the rapist and the non-rapist
   is that the rapist does not find a legitimate
   outlet for his sexual desires and,,therefore,
   turns to rape.

248. Prevost, Earle G. "Statutory Rape: A Growing
     Liberalization." SOUTH CAROLINA LAW
     REVIEW, 18: 254-266, 1966.

   Statutory rape is defined and the elements
   necessary in the prosecution of a statutory
   rape case are presented. The statutory rape
   laws reflect a desire to protect the child
   who is unable to fully understand the act
   and its consequences. The history of this
   concept and the enactment of legislation
   prohibiting statutory rape are discussed.
   Prior sexual activity on the part of the
   victim and the absence of MENS REA on the
   part of the defendant are suggested as
   possible defenses against a charge of
   statutory rape. Prevost recommends two
   possible courses of action to prevent
   injustices in the prosection of statutory
   rape cases.

249. "The Price of Rape." TIME, 108(10): 32,
     September 6, 1976.

   This brief selection discusses various cases
   of rape in which the proprietors of
   establishments where the rapes had occurred
   had been sued for damages by the rape victims.

250. Queen's Bench Foundation. A GUIDE FOR VICTIMS
     OF SEXUAL ASSAULT. San Francisco: Queen's
     Bench Foundation, 1976. 37 pages.

     This pamphlet outlines the procedures that
     victims should follow immediately after a
     sexual assault. Medical procedures,
     police procedures, the court process, victim
     compensation, procedures for filing a civil
     suit or a claim, and possible emotional
     and physical responses to rape are discussed
     in detail. Directed toward women in the
     San Francisco area, this pamphlet lists
     services available to victims, including
     addresses and telephone numbers of rape
     crisis centers, hospitals, law enforcement
     agencies, and other programs to aid the
     victim. A glossary of significant legal
     terms is also provided.

251. Queen's Bench Foundation. RAPE: PREVENTION AND
     RESISTANCE. San Francisco: Queen's Bench
     Foundation, 1976. 125 pages.

     The foundation collected data on rape through
     personal interviews. Aspects of the assault
     itself, the assailant, the victim's feelings
     and thoughts during the assault, force
     employed by the assailant, resistance exerted
     by the victim and the effect of this
     resistance, attitudes toward sexual assault,
     safety precautions learned in childhood and
     childhood experiences of the victim which
     were related to self-assertion and physical
     aggression, and the impact of the assault
     on the victim were studied. Relationships
     were found between the assailants' ethnic
     backgrounds, drinking, drug use, and the
     completion of the assault. Many patterns
     were observed in relation to the relationship
     between offender and victim, the initial
     encounter, the location of the assault,
     and the victim's reactions to the experience.
     The findings of this study show that
     physical resistance or submission does not
     guarentee that the victim will not be
     harmed, and that the effect of physical
     resistance will vary with each circumstance.

However, a significant correlation was found between extreme violence and deterrence.

This work also includes a two page general bibliography on rape.

252. Queen's Bench Foundation. RAPE VICTIMIZATION STUDY. San Francisco: Queen's Bench Foundation, 1975. 118 pages.

The methodology and findings of a rape victimization study conducted in the San Francisco area are presented. The psychological impact of the crime upon the victim, the procedures employed by medical and law enforcement personnel in handling rape complaints, treatment needs of victims, services available to rape victims, and the underreporting of the crime were explored. Following the study, the foundation evaluated and made recommendations to the San Francisco Police Department, the Department of Public Health, District Attorney, and community service agencies. The study recognized the need for public education programs, changes in public attitudes toward rape victims, and the need for legislative reform in the area of rape.

A twenty-page summary is also available.

253. Rada, Richard T. "Alcoholism and Forcible Rape." AMERICAN JOURNAL OF PSYCHIATRY, 132(4): 444-446, April 1975.

Data were collected from the autobiographies of convicted rapists to discover if a correlation existed between alcohol and forcible rape. The findings show a significant association between alcoholism and forcible rape: Thirty-five percent (35%) of the sample was found to be alcoholic, and fifty percent (50%) had been drinking at the time of the offense. Demographic data concerning the alcoholic offenders are also presented.

254. "Rape." THE MEDICO-LEGAL JOURNAL, 44(1): 1-3, 1976.

Central to this editorial is the assumption that a man guilty of rape must possess mens rea (guilty mind). In a 1975 British rape case, the defendant believed that the victim had consented to sexual intercourse and, thus, there was no intent to rape on the part of the defendant. The court pointed out, however, that such a belief claimed by a defendant is not sufficient grounds for an acquittal in a rape case. This editorial discusses this case in detail, highlighting significant issues and recommendations of the court.

255. "Rape." OFF OUR BACKS, 2(7): 8, March 1972.

Rape can take many forms in addition to the type defined by law. This selection discusses other types of rapes, declaring that all men participate in some form of rape, be it physical or verbal, and that rape is an act of power, domination, and exploitation. The author suggests that the type of rape varies with the social class of the rapist, and that most men forcefully control any sexual situation, be it forcible rape or any other heterosexual form of sexual expression. The myth that women are raped because they want to be is also discussed.

256. "Rape: The Experience." WOMEN: A JOURNAL OF LIBERATION, 3(1): 18-19, 1972.

The author relates her experience with rape, emphasizing the reactions of the police to her situation. She states that her feelings of guilt and humiliation were the most damaging consequences of the rape.

257. "The Rape Corroboration Requirement: Repeal
        Not Reform." THE YALE LAW JOURNAL,
        81: 1365-1391, 1972.

    New York State's controversial corroboration
    requirement, long necessary to prove rape
    in New York State, is the subject of this
    article. The history, substance, prevalence,
    and effect of the corroboration requirement
    are examined. Important to this article
    is its discussion of the justifications
    for the existence of a corroboration requirement
    to prove that a rape did occur. These
    justifications include false rape charges,
    and the possibility that the defendant will
    not receive fair legal treatment because
    of the emotional reactions to an accusation
    of rape. Arguements for reform and various
    modifications to a required corroboration
    rule are suggested, concluding that a
    corroboration rule created by the legislature
    should be abandoned in favor of an alternative
    rule, or a substansive modification of the
    present corroboration rule should be affected,
    as had been done in New York State.

258. "Rape Offenders Treatment Program to Begin."
        BIG MAMA RAG, August 1974, page 21.

    The focus of this selection is on the
    evaluation and treatment program for sex
    offenders, as proposed by Dr. Harry Chapman
    of Denver General Hospital. A sex offender
    can be treated by the Colorado courts in
    one of three ways: if found guilty, he can
    be sentenced to a correctional facility;
    he can be sentenced, under the Sexual
    Offenders Act, to a treatment and rehabilitation
    unit; a plea of not guilty by reason of insanity
    can be entered and, if after a psychiatric
    examination the defendant is found to be
    insane, he is placed in a hospital for the
    insane until the hospital staff determines
    that he is "cured." Chapman's program,
    however, establishes instead, a half-way
    house for offenders and provides employment
    for them within the community. Included
    in Chapman's proposal is a plan to evaluate

sex offenders as to their dangerousness
and the likelihood of recidivism in order
to provide appropriate, individualized
treatment.

259. "Rape Prevention Tactics." MS. MAGAZINE,
3(1): 114-115, July 1974.

This selection outlines methods for
protecting one's self against assault.
Procedures for securing one's home against
intrusion, possible "weapons" to be utilized
in the event of an attack, and precautionary
measures to be observed when walking alone
are suggested.

260. "The Rape Wave." NEWSWEEK, 81: 59, January 29,
1973.

The large number of suspected unreported
rapes in New York City prompted the New
York City Police Department to create a
Rape Investigation and Analysis Section,
directed and staffed entirely by female
personnel. The operation of the Rape
Investigation and Analysis Section is
discussed. The director of the unit states
that there has been a substantial increase
in reported rapes since the creation of the
unit. She attributes this increase to
the fact that a victim is able to report
the crime to women detectives and more
comfortably discuss the details of the
assault.

261. "Recent Statutory Developments in the Definition
of Forcible Rape." VIRGINIA LAW REVIEW,
61(7): 1500-1543, November 1975.

The underreporting of rapes, the low rate
of convictions for the crime, and a rise
in the incidence of rape support the notion
that this country's rape laws are inadequate.
The author of this note states that the
difficulty with rape laws can be traced to
the laws' definitions of what constitutes
forcible rape. Attempts to remedy this
definitional inadequacy are analyzed, and

areas with significant definitional problems
are identified and discussed. These problem
areas include: corroboration. the relationship
between the conduct of the victim and that
of the offender, the gradated degrees of
forcible rape, and the requirement of mens rea
in rape cases. In conclusion, this note
examines recent alterations in the content
and focus of rape legislation which catagorize
forcible rape as a type of violent assault.
This new characterization places rape in a
catagory in which standards employed in
other cases of criminal assault must also
be employed in rape cases.

262. Roth, Edwin I. "Emergency Treatment of Raped
      Children." MEDICAL ASPECTS OF HUMAN SEXUALITY,
      6(8): 85-91, August 1972.

      Treating the child victim of rape may involve
      a complex, problematic situation for a
      physician. The victim's physical and
      emotional condition must be considered during
      the examination and the impact of a
      gynecological examination upon a child must
      be recognized. The physician is advised
      to proceed with caution in spite of the fact
      that he may be pressured by parents and
      by law enforcement personnel to perform
      an immediate examination. Roth discusses
      the problems which are typical of most raped
      children, and suggests methods for treating
      them.

263. Rowan, Carl T. and David M. Mazie. "The Terrible
      Trauma of Rape." READER'S DIGEST, 104:
      198-204, March 1974.

      For the victim, the aftermath of a rape
      may be as traumatic as the rape itself.
      Safeguards initiated by law enforcement
      officials and legislatures to protect
      accused rapists from unjust convictions
      have succeeded at the expense of the victim.
      Rowan and Mazie discuss the legal aspects
      of rape, including the stringent safeguards
      written into some rape laws. Offender
      characteristics, medical treatment required

by the victim, methods of prevention for rape, and the development of rape crisis centers to aid the rape victim are also examined.

264. Roy, K.K. "Feelings and Attitudes of Raped Women of Bangladesh Towards Military Personnel of Pakistan." in: Drapko, Israel and Emilio Viano, VICTIMOLOGY: A NEW FOCUS, Volume V. Lexington, Massachusetts: Lexington Books, 1975, pp. 65-72.

Roy emphasizes the cruelty, brutality, and humiliation suffered by the women as the military personnel of Pakistan raped and terrorized the people of Bangladesh. Statistics and details of the crimes are given, and the attitudes of the victims toward the rapes, and toward themselves as rape victims, are discussed.

265. Rubin, Sol. "It's Rape Even If She's Willing." SEXOLOGY, 39: 17-20, September 1972.

A male having sexual intercourse with a female who is, by law, under the age of consent is guilty of statutory rape even though the female consented to the act and no force was involved. In most states, statutory rape is an extremely serious felony which carries severe penalties. Rubin states that, generally, statutory rape laws are "illogical" in that the male is being charged with rape when, in fact, the act committed is not actually rape. In addition, in a case of statutory rape, the male is always considered criminal, even though both parties consented to the act. The rationale behind the enactment of laws governing sexual behavior is also discussed. Rubin concludes by suggesting methods for improving the laws governing sexual behavior.

266. Rush, Florence. "The Sexual Abuse of Children:
     A Feminist Point of View." THE RADICAL
     THERAPIST, pp. 9-10, December 1971.

   The author presents some statistics on the
   incidence of the sexual abuse of children,
   and comments on four case studies made
   during the course of her work with the
   Society for the Prevention of Cruelty to
   Children. The sociological and psychological
   aspects of this form of sexual abuse are
   also discussed.

267. Russell, Diana E.H. THE POLITICS OF RAPE:
     THE VICTIM'S PERSPECTIVE. New York:
     Stein and Day, 1975. 311 pages.

   As the subtitle suggests, Russell speaks
   to the subject of rape from the
   perspective of the rape victim. A large
   portion of this book consists of accounts
   of rape involving twenty-two victims. The
   author also devotes a chapter to interviews
   with rapists, asking these men why they
   raped and what their feelings were toward
   the crime. The book concludes with chapters
   exploring various alternatives and reforms
   to present methods long considered to be
   solutions to the problem of rape. A
   section dealing with rape prevention, as well
   as advice on what procedures a woman should
   follow if she is raped are included.

   This work also includes a seven page general
   bibliography on rape.

268. Sagarin, Edward. "Forcible Rape and the Problem
     of the Rights of the Accused." INTELLECT,
     103(2366): 515-520, May/June 1975.

   The crime of rape is unique among violent
   crimes. The victim may suffer psychological
   as well as physical injuries, and her claim
   of being raped may not be believed. There
   is a low conviction rate for rape, even
   though, frequently, strong evidence points
   to the accused as the perpetrator of the
   crime. Because of this, the women's
   movement has actively demonstrated its

outrage at the way in which rape cases are handled by the police and by the courts. Sagarin feels that the pressure exerted by women's groups may aid the victim of a rape at the expense of the rights of the alleged assailant. False accusations of rape are also discussed, and the conditions under which a false accusation is likely to occur are explored. Guidelines concerning rape accusations are presented, emphasizing the probability of injustice for the accused as a result of suggested reforms.

269. Saperstein, Avalie. "Child Rape Victims and Their Families." in: Schultz, LeRoy G., editor, RAPE VICTIMOLOGY. Springfield, Illinois: Charles C. Thomas, 1975, pp. 274-276.

Major differences exist between the child victim and the adult victim of sexual assaults. These differences must be given consideration when treating the child victim. The need for a constructive response by the parent to the child's situation is seen as being extremely important in helping the child to adjust following the assault. The counseling staff of Women Organized Against Rape in Philadelphia, Pennsylvania has established a procedure for treating the child victim and her parents. This procedure is discussed in detail.

270. Sasko, Helene and Deborah Sesek. "Rape Reform Legislation: Is It the Solution?" CLEVELAND STATE LAW REVIEW, 24(3): 463-503, 1975.

With the incidence of forcible rape rising dramatically, one may expect the rate of prosecution to rise proportionally. In truth, according to Sasko and Sesek, less than fourteen percent (14%) of all reported rapes are successfully prosecuted. Through an analysis of rape statutes of different states, the authors suggest many possible reasons for this low rate of successful prosecutions. The areas of rape legislation

130

in need of reform are discussed, and
recommendations for reform are suggested.
The authors feel that the crime of rape
carries an unreasonably high standard of
proof which burdens the victim unduly and
makes rape prosecution difficult. Also,
the authors state, present rape legislation
does not effectively deter the potential
rapist, nor does it contribute to the
lowering of the high rate of recidivism
among convicted rapists.

271. Savitz, Leonard and Harold I. Lief. "Negro and
White Sex Crime Rates." in: Slovenko, Ralph,
editor, SEXUAL BEHAVIOR AND THE LAW.
Springfield, Illinois: Charles C. Thomas,
1965, pp. 210-230.

This selection focuses on the sex crime
rates of blacks, with the emphasis being
on the sociological and socioeconomic factors
involved in crime causation. The authors
discuss the effect of social class, the
family, sex, and age on the commission of
sex crimes. Differential legal treatment
based on race and existing in the arrest,
the trial, and punishment of an offender
are discussed. The absence of impartial
justice in the legal processing of the
black offender is highlighted.

272. Schiff, Arthur Frederick. "Examining the Sexual
Assault Victim." JOURNAL OF THE FLORIDA
MEDICAL ASSOCIATION, 56(9): 731-739,
September 1969.

In Dade County, Florida, the Medical
Examiner's Office, an autonomous unit, is
responsible for examining sexual assault
victims. The procedures followed by this
unit in examining rape victims, including
the collection of evidence, are discussed.
Rape and sodomy, the most common forms of
sexual assault, are defined and explained.
Schiff emphasizes the fact that the physician
may not make the judegment as to whether
a rape had actually occurred; his function is
to examine the victim and collect evidence for
the judge or the jury to analyze.

273. Schiff, Arthur Frederick. "Rape." MEDICAL ASPECTS
      OF HUMAN SEXUALITY, 6(5): 76-84, May 1972.

      Schiff deals rather generally with the
      problem of rape. After presenting some
      statistics illustrating the extent of the
      problem in the United States, a lengthly
      section concerning the legal definitions
      of rape is presented. The characteristics
      of victims are dealt with quite extensively
      and, although victim-offender relationships
      are discussed, little is said about the
      chatacteristics of the assailants. Schiff
      ends his discussion with an exploration into
      the problem of pretended rapes, and
      suggestions for avoiding a sexual assault.

274. Schiff, Arthur Frederick. "Rape in Foreign
      Countries." MEDICAL TRIAL TECHNIQUE
      QUARTERLY, 20: 66-74, Summer 1973.

      The nature and extent of rape in the countries
      of Greece, Italy, Spain, and Switzerland
      are explored. The author discusses attitudes
      toward rape, the incidence of sexual assault,
      the medical and legal management of the
      victim, and the penalties imposed for the
      crime. After comparing rape in European
      countries with rape in the United States,
      Schiff concludes that the incidence of rape
      is greater in the United States than it is
      in the European countries studied, and
      that the attitudes toward the crime in all
      of the countries observed are similar.

275. Schiff, Arthur Frederick. "Rape in Other
      Countries." MEDICINE, SCIENCE AND THE LAW,
      11(3): 139-143, July 1971.

      Various aspects of the crime of rape in
      other countries are compared and contrasted
      with those in the United States. Attitudes
      toward the crime, the management of the
      victim, and the penalties imposed upon
      offenders are discussed in detail. Schiff
      concludes that the incidence of rape is
      much lower, and the penalties for the crime
      much less severe, in other countries than
      in the United States.

276. Schiff, Arthur Frederick. "A Statistical
          Evaluation of Rape." FORENSIC SCIENCE,
          2(3): 339-349, August 1973.

      Schiff examines the crime of rape with the
      use of official statistics. Age, race,
      and marital status of the victims were noted.
      Offender characteristics considered to be
      significant were age and race. The location
      of the assault, weapons used, the degree
      of injury to the victim, evidence, the
      disposition if cases, and sentences received
      are also discussed. The author concludes
      by recommending that the penalty for rape
      be increased in order for it to act as a
      successful deterrent. He suggests that
      harsher penalties for rape would greatly
      reduce the incidence of the crime.

277. Schiff, Arthur Frederick. "Statistical Features
          of Rape." JOURNAL OF FORENSIC SCIENCES,
          14(1): 102-110, January 1969.

      Rape is difined and the definition is
      explained in detail. The incidence and
      extent of the problem of rape is discussed
      through the use of statistics gathered from
      one hundred consecutive cases of alleged
      rape in Dade County, Florida. Of the
      sample studied, sixty-four percent (64%) of
      the victims were black, and fifty-two percent
      (52%) were unmarried. The ages of the victims
      ranged from four to seventy-three years.
      In reference to the offenders, fifty-eight
      percent (58%) of the cases involved only
      one assailant, and the majority of the
      offenders were black. The locations of the
      offenses, the degree of injury to the victims,
      the credibility of the accusations made
      by the alleged victims, and the apprehension
      and punishment of the offenders are also
      discussed.

278. Schmidt, Peggy. "How to Make Trouble: Rape Crisis
          Centers." MS. MAGAZINE, 2(3): 14-18,
          September 1973.

      Women all across the country have formed
      rape crisis centers to aid the victims of

sexual assault by assisting them with
medical, legal, and psychological problems.
Schmidt discusses the procedures involved
in forming and operating a rape crisis center.
Forming a staff, funding, services to be
offered, and ascertaining what medical and
psychological facilities are available to
the rape victim are among the areas of
immediate concern to women when forming a
rape crisis center. The legal processes
involved in processing a rape complaint by
the police and the courts are discussed in
detail. Suggestions for training volunteers
and publicizing the center are also provided.

279. Schultz, LeRoy G. "The Child as a Sex Victim:
Socio-legal Perspectives." in: Schultz,
LeRoy G., editor, RAPE VICTIMOLOGY.
Springfield, Illinois: Charles C.Thomas,
1975, pp. 257-273.

The social and legal aspects of sexual assaults
on children are discussed. Following an
examination of the incidence of child
victimization and characteristics of child
victims, Schultz discusses the effects of a
sexual assault upon the child victim, and
suggests some implications for treatment.
Professional methods for interviewing the
child victim are also explained. The author
concludes that a child may not have excessive
physical or emotional damage as a result of
the assault, and that most sexual assaults
have no affect on the personality development
of the victim.

280. Schultz, LeRoy G. "Psychotherapeutic and Legal
Approaches to the Sexually Victimized Child."
INTERNATIONAL JOURNAL OF CHILD PSYCHOTHERAPY,
PP. 115-128, 1972.

The incidence of sexual assaults of children
is much greater than is indicated by official
statistics. Schultz states that only about
fifty percent of these crimes are reported
to law enforcement officials. The various
degrees of victimogenesis involved in these
offenses is discussed. Experts feel that

in general, sexual assaults do not seriously
affect the child's psychological adjustments
in childhood or in adult life, but it is
the victim's relationship with the offender
which determines the degree of emotional
or psychological reaction to the offense.
The implications of treatment are explored,
with the emphasis being placed on psychotherapy.

281. Schultz, LeRoy G. RAPE VICTIMOLOGY. Springfield,
        Illinois: Charles C. Thomas, 1975. 405 pages.

        The nineteen selections in this book edited
        by Schultz discuss varied aspects of rape.
        The editor divides this work into six
        main sections, and provides a brief,
        comprehensive introduction to each section.

        This work also includes a ten page general
        bibliography on rape.

282. Schultz, LeRoy G. and Jan DeSavage. "Rape and
        Rape Attitudes on a College Campus."
        in: Schultz, LeRoy G., editor, RAPE VICTIMOLOGY.
        Springfield, Illinois: Charles C. Thomas,
        1975, pp. 77-90.

        This selection is based on a survey conducted
        by the authors, in which single, white males
        and females between the ages of nineteen and
        twenty-four years of age were sampled.
        The purpose of this study was to ascertain
        the most prevalent form of sexual violence
        occurring on a college campus, and as defined
        by law and the students surveyed. The
        authors found that, in general, the students
        surveyed did not understand what actually
        constitutes rape. Students were also
        surveyed concerning victim precipitation,
        ways of expressing consent and non-consent
        in a rape situation, and ways of dealing with
        male's sexual aggression. Schultz and
        DeSavage conclude by recommending changes in
        present practices for dealing with rape on
        many levels. These recommendations include
        more specialized training of personnel,
        increased research in the area of rape, and
        the initiation of good human sexuality courses
        into the colleges academic programs.

283. Schurr, Cathleen. "And Then They Raped the Courts."
     PITTSBURGH FORUM, p. 3, November 26, 1971.

     Society's double standard of sexual behavior
     obviously favors the defendant at the expense
     of the victim during a rape trial. The
     author provides an account of an actual
     rape in support of this observation,
     emphasizing the importance of the victim's
     sexual reputation, either actual or suspected,
     to the verdict handed down by the jury.
     Schurr also discusses the cross-examination
     of a rape victim by the defense attorney,
     and the influence of prevalent myths and
     sexual taboos concerning rape upon the
     operation of the legal process during the
     investigation and trial of a rape case.

284. Schurr, Cathleen. "AP 'Rape Reports' Choked
     Pittsburgh." PITTSBURGH FORUM, p. 6,
     November 5, 1971.

     Rape is the most underreported crime in the
     United States. Factors contributing to the
     underreporting of the crime include: conditioning
     of the female into sex roles, the attitudes of
     law enforcement personnel and the courts toward
     rape and rape victims, and the nature of rape
     laws. In addition to the incidence of rape
     in the United States, Schurr also discusses
     the reporting of incidents of alleged rape
     and other sexual activities which had occurred
     in Pittsburgh a few weeks before this article
     was written.

285. Schurr, Cathleen. "Double Standards Lurk in
     Rape's Shadows." PITTSBURGH FORUM, p. 3,
     November 19, 1971.

     The attitudes of police tend to support
     societal attitudes toward the crime of
     rape. Because of the double standard of
     sexual behavior for males and females, the
     police frequently have difficulty in
     being completely objective when investigating
     a rape complaint. Schurr mentions incidents
     in which the police acted in an unprofessional
     manner when dealing with sex offenses or
     other situations in which sex was involved.

136

The importance of a victim's reactions to
a sexual assault are discussed in detail.
Schurr states that the police expect a
certain reaction from the rape victim,
and if she reacts in a manner which
deviates from these expectations, she
is immediately suspected of placing
a false complaint.

286. Schurr, Cathleen. "Most Defenses Against
Rape 'Outdated'." PITTSBURGH FORUM,
p. 7, December 17, 1971.

Schurr states that most methods
frequently prescribed as preventative
measures against rape are either
ineffective, or they severely restrict a
woman's behavior. This article suggests
measures which may prevent rape or deter
a potential rapist.

287. Schurr, Cathleen. "Rape: The Most
Underreoprted Crime." PITTSBURGH
FORUM, p. 6, November 12, 1971.

The author attempts to explain why rape
is the most underreported crime in the
United States today. Societal attitudes
toward sexual assaults are discussed,
including the prevailing double standard
of sexual behavior for men and women.
Rape in predominantly black, and
predominantly white, sections of Pittsburgh
are explored, emphasizing the fact that
the lower incidence of rape in the
predominantly white areas may be attributed
to the fact that sexual assaults are
least likely to be reported by victims
living in these areas. Schurr concludes
by stating that "every girl's sexual
heritage" is laced with feelings of
humiliation and fear, and that the reluctance
of women to report sexual assaults may be
attributed, in part, to this type of sexual
indoctrination which had been initiated
in childhood.

288. Schurr, Cathleen. "Rape: The Victim's
      'Required' Behavior." PITTSBURGH
      FORUM, p. 6, December 10, 1971.

      It is believed that a rape victim must
      react to the assault according to a standard
      of "legal required behavior." Schurr
      discusses what this means to the rape victim
      and the effect of this behavior upon the
      court during a rape trial.

289. Schurr, Cathleen. "Some Notes on Sex and
      Rape Mythology." PITTSBURGH FORUM,
      p. 3, December 3, 1971.

      Society perpetrates certain myths concerning
      the proscribed sexual behavior of women
      and men, and rape, which may be the result
      of deviations, by women, from these
      proscriptions. The influence of these
      myths upon the reactions of the public
      toward the problem of rape is the focus
      of discussion in this article. The
      concepts of the "rape-prone male" and the
      female as the sexual property of the male
      are among the areas explored.

290. Schwartz, Barry. "The Effect in Philadelphia
      of Pennsylvania's Increased Penalties for
      Rape and Attempted Rape." THE JOURNAL
      OF CRIMINAL LAW, CRIMINOLOGY, AND POLICE
      SCIENCE, 59(4): 509-515, 1968.

      In 1966, the Pennsylvania Legislature
      passed a bill which provided for increased
      penalties for rape in the state of
      Pennsylvania. The author conducted a study
      in Philadelphia to determine if the
      increased penalties for rape would succeed
      in deterring the potential rapist, thus
      significantly reducing the number of rapes
      occurring in that city. Rapes and attempted
      rapes occurring in Philadelphia from
      1958-1966 are discussed. A detailed
      analysis of rape and attempted rape in the
      city of Philadelphia for the year 1966 is
      presented. Schwartz found that the
      imposition of stronger penalties for rape

138

apparently did not act to deter potential
rapists, since the rate of rape in the
city of Philadelphia did not decrease.

291. Schwendinger, Julia R. and Herman Schwendinger.
"Rape Myths: In Legal, Theoretical, and
Everyday Practice." CRIME AND SOCIAL
JUSTICE: A JOURNAL OF RADICAL CRIMINOLOGY,
1: 18-26, Spring-Summer 1974.

The crime of rape is complicated by the
perpetuation of numerous myths concerning
the offense. These myths influence the
attitudes of the public and of law
enforcement personnel toward rape and
rape victims. The authors discuss five
of the most prevalent and damaging of these
of these myths and the legal and moral
issues which result from them. The issues
of consent, resistance, sex role stereotypes,
and class differences are discussed in detail.
The development of programs for treating
the physical, emotional, and psychological
injuries sustained by the rape victim are explored.
The authors conclude by advocating a change
in the oppressive class system which exists
in the United States today. They state that
crimes of violence are the result of the
capitalistic system, and that in order to
end the rise of violent crime, this country
should adopt a socialist type of political
economy.

292. Sebba, Leslie and Sorel Cahan. "Sex Offenses:
The Genuine and the Doubted Victim." in:
Drapkin, Israel and Emilio Vivano,
VICTIMOLOGY: A NEW FOCUS, Volume V.
Lexington, Massachusetts: Lexington Books,
1975, pp. 29-43.

This selection focuses on the sex offenses
committed in Israel. The authors analyzed
data obtained from police files and
classified it according to the processing
of cases by police, the district attorneys,
and the court systems. The sex, age, and
marital status of the offenders and the
victims were noted, as was the type of

offense, the relationship between the victim
and the offender, the prior criminal record
of the offender, and the time and location
of the incident. The outcome of each
complaint was analyzed. The authors
conclude that the criminal justice system's
determination of who is the genuine victim,
the complainant or the offender, and, thus,
who is responsible for the crime, is
influenced by many factors, either germaine
or external to the case.

293. Selkin, James. "Rape." PSYCHOLOGY TODAY,
        8(8): 71-75, January 1975.

Rape can have a grave psychological impact
on both the offender and the victim.
From the author's own clinical experiences
with rapists, he concludes that intimidation
of the victim by the rapist is "a necessary
precondition to rape." Ways in which women
resist their assailants are explored,
emphasizing the psychological condition
of the victim during the assault. Ways
in which a rapist chooses his victim and
suggestions for rape prevention are
presented. Selkin also discusses the
incidence of murder resulting from a sexual
assault, reasons why men rape, and insights
into the diagnosis of a man as a potential
rapist.

294. Shaffer, Helen B. "Crime of Rape." EDITORIAL
        RESEARCH REPORTS, 1(3): 42-60,
        January 19, 1972.

This article is divided into three sections.
The first section deals generally with rape,
emphasizing the sociological and psychological
aspects of the crime. Underreporting by
victims to law enforcement personnel,
criticisms by women's liberation advocates
of the handling of rape complaints, and
physical and psychological injury to the
victim are among the topics discussed.
The second section focuses on the conditions
most conducive to rape, and on the psychology

of the rapist and the rapist-murderer.
The author also briefly explores the
question of pornography as a causal factor
in the commission of a sex crime. The
final section of this article discusses
sexual offenses and the legal process.
The issues of corroboration and
resistance standards are explored and
sentencing and treatment of convicted
rapists are discussed. The section concludes
with a discussion of self-defense and rape
prevention.

295.   Shah, Diane K. "Women Attack Rape Justice."
         THE NATIONAL OBSERVER, 10(40): 1,
         October 9, 1971.

In the past, the defendant in a rape case had
been treated unjustly by the legal system.
Today, according to this article, the
situation is quite different, and the scales
of justice are tipped to favor the
defendant at the expense of the victim.
Myths surrounding the crime of rape support
the unsubstantiated, contributory role of
the victim in the crime. The need for
revision in rape laws and in penalties for
committing the crime are discussed. Shah
states that women's attitudes toward rape
are changing, and that their anger over
the crime is being turned into constructive
action to prevent rapes from occurring.
Preventative measures to reduce the
probability of rape are suggested.

296.   Shaw, Bernice L. "When the Problem is Rape. . . ."
         R.N. MAGAZINE, 35: 27-29, April 1972.

Part of the responsibility of the nurse
who treats a rape victim is to objectively
observe and record the victims condition,
and to provide counseling when necessary.
Shaw outlines the procedures established by
the American College of Obstetrics and
Gynecology for examining sexual assault
victims. The psychological reactions of
the victim to the rape are also discussed,
emphasizing the implications of these
reactions for treatment by medical personnel.

297. Sheehy, Gail. "Nice Girls Don't Get Into
          Trouble." NEW YORK, 4: 26-30,
          February 15, 1971.

          The reactions of law enforcement personnel
          to rape victims, and the subsequent reactions
          of the victims to the attitudes of the police,
          are discussed. Rape victims who had
          attended a conference on rape held in New
          York City related their experiences with
          rape and with the police. Most victims
          expressed feelings of guilt and responsibility
          for the assault. It was felt that the
          attitudes of disbelief, indifference, and
          ridicule expressed by the police had
          contributed to the victim's feelings of
          guilt. Sheehy states that it is the victim
          who is treated as a criminal, while efforts
          are made to protect the accused against the
          possibility of a false accusation of rape.

298. Sheldon, Ann. "Rape: A Solution." WOMEN: A
          JOURNAL OF LIBERATION, 3(1): 22, 1972.

          Sheldon suggests that since the number of
          actual rapes is so much greater than the
          rate of reported rapes, and the rate of
          convictions for forcible rape is so
          small, the legal system is not effective
          in preventing or deterring rape. Sheldon
          suggests alternative solutions.

299. Shelly, Martha. "How It Works in L.A. . . . . "
          MS. MAGAZINE, 2(3): 16, September 1973.

          Shelley provides a detailed description
          of the development and operation of an
          anti-rape squad in LosAngeles, California.
          The Anti-Rape Commission, a project
          developed to educate or re-educate the public,
          police, welfare workers, medical personnel,
          and others concerning rape and the treatment
          of rape victims is also discussed.

300. Sheppard, David I. and others. "Rape Reduction:
A Citywide Program." in: Walker, Marcia J.
and Stanley L. Brodsky, editors, SEXUAL
ASSAULT. Lexington, Massachusetts:
Lexington Books, 1976, pp. 169-175.

The need for special law enforcement
measures for dealing with rape is
recognized and discussed by the authors.
The victim's psychological reaction to the
crime, the victim's reluctance to report the
crime promptly to the police, the collection
and identification of physical evidence,
the low rate of prosecution and conviction
for rape cases, and prevention of rape are
noted as problem areas for law enforcement
personnel. The problem of rape in Denver,
Colorado is analyzed and that city's rape
reduction program is explained. The
authors conclude that cities must study their
own patterns of rape and structure a program
to coincide with each city's particular
needs.

301. Shook, Howard C. "Revitalized Methods Needed
for Investigation of Rape Complaints."
THE POLICE CHIEF, 40(12): 14-15,
December 1973.

Shook emphasizes the need for change in
methods of police investigation of rape
cases. Criticism of police methods in
dealing with the victim and the crime in
in general has been made by women's groups
and the public. This criticism, together
with statistics from the Federal Bureau
of Investigation's Uniform Crime Reports,
which show that rape is the most rapidly
increasing violent crime and the most
underreported, support Shook's observation
of a need for change in police methods.
The attempt of one police department to
analyze its operations in light of these
facts and criticisms is presented. It was
found that the present methods used by this
particular police department were outdated

and inadequate to handle the reality of
the crisis situation involved in forcible
rape, and recommendations for improvement
are made.

302. Shopper, Moisy. "Psychiatric and Legal Aspects
of Statutory Rape, Pregnancy and Abortion
in Juveniles." THE JOURNAL OF PSYCHIATRY
AND LAW, 1(3): 275-295, Fall 1973.

Following a general discussion of the legal
status of minors under the criminal and
civil laws, Shopper focuses his attention
on statutory rape and compulsory pregnancy.
Compulsory pregnancy, whether resulting
from rape or the difficulty in obtaining
contraceptives, is defined as an
unwanted pregnancy in which the woman
is forced, by external factors, to carry
the child to term. It is argued that
if a female minor willingly participates
in intercourse, a compulsory pregnancy
cannot result. The opposite view states
that even though the pregnancy itself is
not compulsory, being forced to carry
the unwanted child to term may be
compulsory. The problem of consent for
abortions for minors is discussed.
Shopper concludes by saying that contraception
and abortion are not readily accessible
to a minor, and minors are often forced
to give birth to unwanted children. He
advocates the enactment of medical
emancipation statutes which would permit
abortions for minors without requiring
parental consent.

303. Shultz, Gladys. "Society and the Sex Criminal."
READER'S DIGEST, 89: 139-146, November
1966.

The author, a victim of attempted rape,
discusses her experience with the legal
system following the arrest of the
assailant. Following a discussion of
the scope of rape in this country, the
validity of statistics concerning sex
crimes is questioned, with plea bargaining

and underreporting suggested as factors
contributing to this invalidity. The
psychology of the sex offender, the
influence of family life upon the
commission of the crime, and methods
employed for treating the sex criminal
are also discussed. Shultz concludes by
mentioning reforms enacted by some states
for the treatment of sex offenders.

304.   Shultz, Gladys. "What Sex Offenders Say About
       Pornography." READER'S DIGEST, 99:
       53-57, July 1971.

       Attempts have been made to establish a
       definite relationship between pornography
       and sex crimes. In an effort to discover
       if there is, indeed, a relationship
       between sex crimes and pornography, the
       author interviewed convicted sex offenders.
       About one-half of the respondents denied
       any influence of pornography on their
       attitudes toward sex. It is the author's
       opinion, however, that since so many of
       the respondents did implicate pornography
       as an influence for their criminal activity,
       a relationship between the two is probable.

305.   Sidney, Nathan T. and Francis J. Stolarz.
       "A Proposed 'Dangerous Sex Offender' Law."
       AMERICAN JOURNAL OF PSYCHIATRY, 130(7):
       765-768, July 1973.

       The amount of attention given to sex offenses
       has not prompted the passage of completely
       effective legislation. The laws governing
       the behavior of the sex offender are
       frequently subjected to misinterpretation
       and abuse. Sidney and Stolarz propose
       legislative reform which would eliminate
       this abuse by clearly defining all aspects
       of the law, and making the committment
       requirements more stringent in order to
       commit to a treatment center only the offenders
       who are most dangerous to society.

306. Slovenko, Ralph, editor. SEXUAL BEHAVIOR AND
THE LAW. Springfield, Illinois: Charles
C. Thomas, 1965. 886 pages.

This book discusses a variety of sexual
behaviors and the laws governing them.
The topics discussed include: prostitution,
rape, sodomy, homosexuality, pornography,
marriage, incest, sexual homicide, and
sexual activities involving children.
Slovenko provides a comprehensive
introduction to each topic. In his
conclusion to the general introduction,
the editor states that many laws governing
sexual behavior are unnecessary, and
suggests revision of these laws.

307. Smith, Cyril J. "History of Rape and Rape
Laws." WOMEN LAWYERS JOURNAL, 60:
188-191, Fall 1974.

Following a brief history of rape, Smith
discusses the laws which have governed
rape from the seventeenth century, B.C.
until the present. The punishments
imposed for rape during various periods
of history are also discussed.

308. Smith, J.C. "The Heilbron Report." THE
CRIMINAL LAW REVIEW, 1976: 97-106,
February 1976.

Smith outlines the report of the Heilbron
Committee, and provides commentary on
its proposals. The report of the
Heilbron Committee, established as a
result of the decision of the House of
Lords in a rape case, involves the question
of criminal responsibility. The
implementation of this report would affirm
the decision reached in the rape case, and
significantly reform the laws pertaining
to rape. In the rape case which led to
the establishment of the committee, the
court held that if a man believes a
woman to be consenting to sexual intercourse,
whether or not she actually is, the man is
not guilty of rape because he had no
intention of committing a crime and is,

146

therefore, not responsible according to
the precepts of criminal law, for a
crime. The Heilbron Committee recommends
that if the law requires proof of intent,
the actual intention of the defendant
must be proved. The committee feels that
its decision strengthens the law against
rape, and that it has important implications
for criminal law in general.

309. Smith, J.Y. "The Rape Victim's Dilemma: How
to React?" THE WASHINGTON POST, p. E-1,
December 2, 1972.

According to the law pertaining to rape,
a victim must, in some way, resist her
assailant for the act to be considered
rape. The victim is faced with a problem:
if she actively resists her assailant, she
may provoke additional harm to her person,
and if she does not resist, she greatly
reduces the possibility that her assailant
will be convicted of the offense in a
court of law. Smith discusses a rape
case in which resistance was an important
issue, and refers to statements made by
Herbert B. Hoffman, the United States
attorney who had prosecuted the case.
Hoffman states that resistance can be
substantiated in a court of law if the
following considerations are met: the
offense is promptly reported, a medical
examination reveals physical damage,
the victim's clothes are torn, the victim
is experiencing psychological or emotional
trauma. Smith concludes by presenting
suggestions for women to avoid potential
rape situations.

310. Snelling, H.A. "What is Non-Consent (in Rape)?"
in: Schultz, LeRoy, editor, RAPE VICTIMOLOGY.
Springfield, Illinois: Charles C. Thomas,
1975, pp. 157-163.

The question of consent is discussed with
the aid of relevant court decisions. The
question of a woman's mental decision not
always agreeing with her conduct in a
particular situation is raised. The author

acknowledges the possibility of a woman
physically submitting to sexual intercourse
as a result of a threat or out of genuine
fear for her physical safety. Cases of
consent in gang rapes is also discussed,
the issue being that the victim may
consent to one act without consenting
to the subsequent ones. The law in theory
not always agreeing with the law in practice
is noted. The author concludes by saying
that a woman must make a deliberate effort
to make her resistance understood by her
assailant. If her assailant then proceeds
with the act, he is subject to the
penalties for rape as imposed by law.

311. Snelling, H.A. "What is Rape?" THE AUSTRALIAN
JOURNAL OF FORENSIC SCIENCES, 211: 22-30,
September 1969.

Various definitions of rape are presented
from an historical perspective. The author
comments on these definitions, citing the
main elements necessary for a crime to be
considered rape, as they evolved from
common law. The need for a clear, concise
definition and understanding of the
question of consent in an alleged rape
is emphasized.

312. Soothill, Keith and Anthea Jack. "How Rape
is Reported." NEW SOCIETY, 32(663):
702-704, June 19, 1975.

The coverage given to rape cases by the
British press is explored. In examining
the number of rape cases reported by five
major newspapers and by the national press
during 1951, 1961, and 1971, the authors
note the low proportion of rape cases which
had been reported in the national press,
stating that although a good number of rape
cases receive some publicity, only a very
small proportion of these receive sustained
coverage. After examining the rape
reports in national newspapers, certain
patterns emerged as to the demeanor of

statements made about the victim, the
presence of "gratutious" remarks, and
the general standards in which rape cases
are reported.

313. Steinem, Gloria.   "But What Do We Do With Our
        Rage?"   MS. MAGAZINE, 3(11): 51, May 1975.

        Citing the Joanne Little and Inez Garcia
        cases as examples, Steinem questions the
        justice in convicting women of first degree
        murder for killing their assailants.   Is
        rape so great an outrage that women must
        react so violently against it?   The pain,
        humiliation, and trauma suffered by the
        victim are evidence of the need for
        some kind of reaction.   As was the case
        with Garcia and Little, victims reacted
        against violence with violence--a reaction
        unexpected from women.   This article
        raises the question: "Under what conditions
        is a violent reaction to sexual attack
        justified?"   Although no answer is
        provided, Steinem states that women must
        understand the way in which the legal
        system operates in cases such as these,
        and definite plans for change must be
        formulated if any reforms are to be
        made.

314. Sullivan, Gail Bernice.   "Rape and Its Neglected
        Victims."   SAN FRANCISCO CHRONICLE, p. B-8,
        April 9, 1972.

        Sullivan relates portions of a discussion
        which took place during a women's
        meeting in San Francisco.   Women discuss
        their experiences with rape, suggesting
        socialization as a justification, if
        one must be given, for the crime.

315. Sutherland, Sandra and Donald J. Scherl.
"Patterns of Response Among Victims of
Rape." AMERICAN JOURNAL OF ORTHOPSYCHIATRY,
40(3): 503-511, April 1970.

Women who move to low income neighborhoods
from middle income ones are subjected to
certain risks, one of which is rape.
The authors studied thirteen victims of
rape, ranging in age from eighteen to
twenty-four years, who had a history of
strong psychological health. Most of the
victims had been seen by the authors within
forty-eight hours after the assault. The
purpose of this study was to discover
"a specific predictable sequence of
responses to rape," and to create a crisis
intervention and guidance program for rape
victims. Three phases of reactions by
victims to rape were identified, and each
phase is discussed in detail. The authors
conclude that a definite response pattern
had emerged. The recognition by treatment
personnel of such a predictable pattern
of response enables the establishment of
more effective crisis intervention programs
for rape victims.

316. Sutherlin, Jerrilee. "Indiana's Rape Shield
Law: Conflict With the Confrontation
Clause?" INDIANA LAW REVIEW, 9(2):
418-440, January 1976.

This article examines Indiana's rape shield law,
and the confrontation clause in the United
States Constitution, in order to determine
whether the rape shield law is in conflict
with the confrontation clause. The
confrontation clause contained in the
fourteenth amendment to the United States
Constitution guarentees a defendant the
right to confront witnesses called to testify
against him during a trial. Indiana's rape
shield law prohibits a victim's past sexual
history from being admitted into evidence
during a rape trial. Referring to a 1974
United States Supreme Court decision in
which both the confrontation clause and

a state shield law came into conflict, Sutherlin concludes that the Indiana statute could be properly utilized without denying the defendant his constitutional rights, depending upon the "judicious use" of the statute by the trial judge.

317. Symonds, Martin. "The Rape Victim: Psychological Patterns of Response." THE AMERICAN JOURNAL OF PSYCHOANALYSIS, 36(1): 27-34, 1976.

The author states that in order to assess the reactions of victims to the crime of rape, rape must be viewed not as a sexual act, but as a crime of violence. Typical patterns followed by offenders in committing violent crimes are presented, emphasizing the element of terror employed to insure compliance on the part of the victim. The psychology of rapists is discussed in detail with the aid of case studies. Victim responses demonstrate "traumatic psychological infantilism" in which helplessness plays a major role. The rape victim submits to her assailant in hopes of inhibiting his aggression. Out of fear and terror, she also exhibits regressive behavior and generally isolates herself from whatever methods of safety may be available to her. Symonds states that sympathetic responses by police personnel immediately following a sexual assault may greatly reduce the psychological trauma experienced by the victim.

318. Szumski, Gerald J. "A New Law Shields Rape Victims' Private Lives." THE NATIONAL OBSERVER, 13(21): 15, May 25, 1974.

This selection discusses a bill, by the Iowa Legislature, which prohibits a victim's past sexual history from being submitted into evidence during a rape trial unless the information is directly relevant to the case. This same bill also repealed the law requiring corroboration to prove rape. It is hoped that this new bill will encourage more victims to report rapes and prosecute their assailants.

319. Taylor, Angela. "The Rape Victim: Is She Also
     the Unintended Victim of the Law?" THE
     NEW YORK TIMES, p. 52, June 15, 1971.

     Laws governing rape are extremely controversal.
     Taylor explores New York State's rape laws
     with the aid of opinions from prominent
     New York State legislators and victim
     accounts of actual rapes. The attitudes
     of the police are briefly discussed and
     methods for preventing rape are suggested.

320. Thompson, Sandra. "Gang Rape: Why It's
     Increasing." SEXOLOGY, 41(8): 16-19,
     March 1975.

     Thompson states that the incidence of group
     rape is rising faster than that of rape
     by a single offender. This increase is
     seen as a response by men who feel
     threatened by the sexually aggressive
     women produced by the Women's Liberation
     Movement. The psychology of group rapists
     is discussed, and a typical case is described.
     The author concludes by suggesting
     precautions which may help to prevent rape.

321. Tonry, Richard A. "Statutory Rape: A Critique."
     LOUISIANA LAW REVIEW, 26(1): 105-117,
     December 1965.

     The laws governing the crime of statutory
     rape are examined. With the aid of the
     English Sexual Offenses Act, the American
     Law Institute's Model Penal Code, and a
     number of significant court decisions, Tonry
     discussed the concept of operative consent
     as being central to determining responsibility
     in statutory rape cases. He concludes that
     if a female consents to sexual intercourse
     and fully understands her participation in
     the act, her age should be irrelevant
     and the male should not be accused of rape.
     Thus, each statutory rape case should be
     decided on the facts of the particular case,
     and the principle of operative consent
     should be allowed as a defense for rape
     in a court of law.

322. Tweedie, Jill. "Rape: Why Is the Woman Always
     to Blame?" THE WASHINGTON POST, p. G-10,
     March 26, 1972.

     Some common myths concerning rape are
     discussed. Tweedie states that rape is
     a uniquely male crime and that it is the
     responsibility of the male to justify
     and defend it. It is implied that the
     myths concerning rape are perpetuated
     for this reason.

323. "Victims of Rape." BRITISH MEDICAL JOURNAL,
     1(5951): 171-172, January 25, 1975.

     Procedures followed by medical personnel
     in dealing with rape victims are
     explained in detail. The legal issues
     involved in such an examination are also
     discussed. In addition, this selection
     briefly mentions the establishment of
     rape crisis centers and similar organizations
     to aid the victims of sexual assaults.

324. Voskuhl, John E. "Criminal Law-- Rape--
     Death Penalty--Eighth Amendment Prohibition
     Against Cruel and Unusual Punishments
     Forbids Execution When the Victim's Life
     Is Neither Taken Nor Endangered."
     CINCINNATI LAW REVIEW, 40(2): 396-401,
     Summer 1971.

     In the case of Ralph v. Warden, 438 F.2d
     786 (4th cir. 1970), the United States
     Court of Appeals held that, in this case,
     the death penalty constituted cruel and
     unusual punishment as prohibited by the
     eighth amendment to the United States
     Constitution, since the victim's life was
     neither taken nor endangered. In addition
     to the case of Ralph v. Warden, other rape
     cases in which the death penalty had been
     an issue are discussed. In the case of
     Ralph v. Warden, two factors were
     instrumental in the determination by the
     court that the death penalty was
     disproportionate to the crime of rape in
     this particular case. Although these

factors-- the fact that the death penalty
is seldom imposed in most states, and
that most rapists are sentenced to prison
and not to death--reflect current trends,
there are some states in which the death
penalty is still considered to be an
appropriate sentence for rape, since any
rape can result in physical, mental, or
emotional harm to the victim.

325. Walker, Mae. "Rape and the Harlem Woman:
'She Asked for It'--Or Did She?"
MAJORITY REPORT, 4(9): 1, August 22, 1974.

A coalition of women's groups in New York
City who were interested in rape prevention
met with the Police Department's Sex Crime
Prevention Unit in order to reach women
who had not reported the crime. Walker
briefly discusses this meeting, focusing
on the special problems of black and third
world women who seek help following a
sexual assault. The author also mentions
the attitudes of some of the males present
concerning rape and rape victims.

326. Walker, Marcia J. and Stanley L. Brodsky,
editors. SEXUAL ASSAULT. Lexington,
Massachusetts: Lexington Books, 1976.
186 pages.

Many aspects of rape are discussed in this
book. The authors of the selections
are professionals who have worked with
rape or other sexual assaults in some
capacity. The introduction to the book
briefly summarizes the salient points of
each selection, in addition to stating
the authors' objectives in compiling the
book.

327. Washburn, R. Bruce. "Rape Law: The Need for
Reform." NEW MEXICO LAW REVIEW, 5(2):
279-309, May 1975.

The Criminal Sexual Conduct Act enacted
by the New Mexico Legislature in 1975,

is the subject of this article. According to this new statute, the degree of the felony depends upon the degree of harm caused to the victim, either physically or psychologically. This statute makes any type of forced sexual behavior criminal, the most severe behavior being sexual penetration of any kind. Forcible rape is discussed in light of this new statute, as are the rules of evidence to prove a crime of rape. The issues of corroboration and character evidence are explored in detail. The author concludes by saying that the new statute brings sexual crimes into a rational perspective by making any sexual act criminal if it does not involve a free choice. He does feel, however, that reform of rape laws is still needed if a victim is to be given the advantages of presumption of innocence and the inadmissability of irrelevant evidence afforded her assailant during the trial.

328. Wasserman, Michelle. "Rape: Breaking the
        Silence." THE PROGRESSIVE, 37(11):
        19-23, November 1973.

        Rape crisis centers are being formed across
        the country to aid rape victims and to
        give them an opportunity to discuss their
        experiences with rape--experiences which
        have traditionally gone undiscussed. The
        establishment and operation of various
        rape crisis centers are explained, and
        their role in "breaking the silence"
        surrounding the crime of rape is emphasized.
        The author also presents suggestions
        from various rape crisis centers concerning
        self-defense and rape prevention.

329. Wecht, Cyril and Wellon D. Collom. "Medical
        Evidence in Alleged Rape." LEGAL MEDICINE
        ANNUAL 1969. New York: Appleton-Century
        Crofts, 1969, pp. 269-285.

        The authors discuss the collection and
        examination of medical evidence in a rape

case. In depth discussions of the physical examination of the victim, physical evidence which assists in identifying the assailant, the physical examination of a suspected rapist, and the examination of materials collected from the site of the assault and from all parties involved are provided.

330. Weddington, Sarah. "Rape Law in Texas: H.B. 284 and the Road to Reform." AMERICAN JOURNAL OF CRIMINAL LAW, 4(1): 1-14, Winter 1975-1976.

The Legislative Council of the Texas Legislature identified areas where reform legislation was possible concerning rape. The two primary areas of concern dealt with the redefining of criminal sexual acts, and increasing the rate of reporting rapes and convicting rapists. House Bill 284, which introduces legislation in these areas, is presented as it was originally proposed and introduced. The development of the final draft of the bill is also discussed.

331. Weis, Kurt and Sandra S. Borges. "Victimology and Rape: The Case of the Legitimate Victim." ISSUES IN CRIMINOLOGY, 8(2): 71-115, Fall 1973.

Victimization as a product of various social processes is discussed. The legitimate victim of a crime is one who has successfully passed through the social processes involved in creating a victim. The legitimate victim of a rape is one who poses no danger to the offender because she cannot effectively relate her experience to law enforcement personnel and is, therefore, unable to successfully accuse and prosecute her assailant. Rape is discussed from an interactionist perspective, focusing on the victim-offender relationship. The importance of viewing this dyadic encounter as it is interpreted by the parties involved is emphasized. The socialization processes of preparing women to be victims

of rape and men to be perpetrators of the
crime are discussed in detail from a
functionalist perspective. The authors
conclude with some predictions concerning
rape in the immediate future, emphasizing
the possible effects of the sexual
revolution and the women's movement on
the incidence of rape.

332. Weis, Kurt and Sandra Weis. "Victimology and
the Justification of Rape." in: Drapkin,
Israel and Emilio Viano, editors,
VICTIMOLOGY: A NEW FOCUS, Volume V.
Lexington, Massachusetts: Lexington Books,
1975, pp. 3-27.

Following a brief discussion of the study
of victimology, Weis and Weis describe the
socialization of victims, emphasizing the
process of sex role socialization and
its importance to the concept of the role
of a rape victim. The socialization
process of offenders compliments the process
of victim socialization by creating the
role of the aggressive male, and providing
a definite association between aggression
and sexuality. The authors proceed to
discuss rape from a symbolic interactionist
perspective, focusing on socialization
processes and common stereotypes as
justifications for rape, be it an actual
or symbolic act. The psychological trauma
experienced by the rape victim, and the
trauma involved in her efforts to relate
the experience to others are presented.
The authors conclude with a discussion of
rape in light of the cultural system in
which the crime occurs, including the
concepts of justifiable rape, the legitimate
victim, and victim precipitation.

333. Weiss, Edward H. and others. "The Mental
Health Committee: Report of the Subcommittee
on the Problem of Rape in the District of
Columbia." MEDICAL ANNALS OF THE DISTRICT
OF COLUMBIA, 41: 703-704, November 1972.

The authors discuss procedures followed by
departments when a woman reports a rape

157

in the District of Columbia. Recommendations
for the improvement of services to rape
victims are made to the specific agencies
involved in each stage of the processing
and investigation of a rape case.

334, Welch, Deborah. "Criminal Procedure--Instruction
to Jury that Rape is Easy to Charge and
Difficult to Disprove is No Longer to be
Given." TEXAS TECH LAW REVIEW, 7: 732-737,
Spring 1976.

In the case of State v. Feddersen, 230 N.W.2d
510 (Iowa 1975), the Iowa Supreme Court ruled
that the instruction to the jury that, "The
charge of rape against a person is easy to
make, difficult to prove, and more difficult
to disprove," was no longer to be given
because it imposed a stricter test of
credibility on the victim of rape than on
the victim of any other offense. The court
also ruled that the instruction was not
actually a statement of law and was,
therefore, inappropriate as a charge to
the jury by the judge. Welch also discusses
this instruction as it is used (or as it
is prohibited from use) in other states.
She concludes that the decision reached
by the Iowa Supreme Court may provide a
base for similar decisions in other courts,
and that such decisions may render better
treatment of the rape victim in the
courtroom.

335. Werner, Arnold. "Rape: Interruption of the
Therapeutic Process by External Stress."
PSYCHOTHERAPY: THEORY, RESEARCH AND
PRACTICE, 9(4): 349-351, Winter 1972.

The effect of rape on psychotherapy is
explored. The author presents the case of
a woman patient undergoing psychotherapy,
who is forcibly raped. The rape altered
therapy by causing severe grief reactions,
and reducing the patient to a dependent
state. It is suggested that the rape may
make real the victim's rape fantasy, thus
causing her to feel guilt and responsibility

for the assault. Werner states that although the rape remains a significant event in the victim's life, it does not become a determining factor, as long as the victim is discouraged from centering her life around the rape.

336. Wesolowski, James J. "Indicia of Consent? A Proposal for Change to the Common Law Rule Admitting Evidence of a Rape Victim's Character for Chastity." LOYOLA UNIVERSITY LAW JOURNAL, 7(1): 118-140, Winter 1976.

The author cites the need for a reevaluation of the common law rule which allows the admissibility of the victim's prior sexual history as evidence in a rape trial when the defendant is alleging consent on the part of the prosecutrix. The development of this rule is presented and the rule is evaluated with the the Illinois rule as an example. The constitutional implications of limiting the use of this rule are considered. Some changes and modifications in the rule are proposed, and the necessity of affecting change in this area is emphasized.

337. "When a Woman is Attacked." in: Schultz, LeRoy, editor, RAPE VICTIMOLOGY. Springfield, Illinois: Charles C. Thomas, 1975, pp. 13-18.

A woman describes her rape experience, including the medical and legal procedures which followed the assault. The account is followed by a brief commentary on rape, which focuses on the opinion that rape is the safest crime that a man can commit because it is a crime which is seldom reported and, if it is reported, the alleged assailant is seldom convicted.

338. Williams, Arthur Hyatt. "Rape-Murder."
      in: Slovenko, Ralph, editor, SEXUAL
      BEHAVIOR AND THE LAW. Springfield,
      Illinois: Charles C. Thomas, 1965,
      pp. 563-577.

      With the aid of case studies, the author
      describes the unconscious motives which
      cause a man to commit rape and murder.
      There are two types of forces acting upon
      a person and causing him to commit rape,
      and the severity of the act depends upon
      the combination of these two forces.
      Williams states that the objective in
      the treatment of the violent sexual offender
      is to reduce the destructive forces which
      cause him to commit violent sexual acts
      against women, and the eventual integration
      of violent, destructive urges with
      non-destructive ones.

339. Williams, J.E. Hall. "The Neglect of Incest:
      A Criminologist's View." in: Drapkin,
      Israel and Emilio Viano, editors,
      VICTIMOLOGY: A NEW FOCUS, Volume IV.
      Lexington, Massachusetts: Lexington
      Books, 1975, pp. 191-196.

      Less than one-half of the cases of incest
      reported to the British police are
      prosecuted and convicted, and most offenders
      sentenced are soon eligible for parole.
      The author studied sixty-eight cases which
      were considered for parole. In this study,
      general offender and victim characteristics
      emerged, in addition to some conclusions
      concerning incest. Williams states that
      incest is too often neglected, and that
      more research is needed in order to
      understand the contributory roles of the
      victims, offenders, and other members of
      the family to the act.

340. Willis, Ellen. "Rape on Trial." ROLLING STONE,
      #194, pp. 38-41, August 28, 1975.

      Willis presents an account of an actual
      rape case in which the assailant was
      found not guilty of the crime by a jury.

The victim's emotional and psychological condition following the trial eventually led to a suicide attempt and a month in a psychiatric hospital. The case is presented in detail, beginning with the victim's initial encounter with the assailant, and ending with her release from a psychiatric hospital. Willis also mentions that before the assault, the victim had been very psychologically healthy. In addition to the psychological condition of the victim, the process involved in prosecuting an alleged rapist, and societal attitudes toward rape and rape victims as reflected in the verdict of the jury and the responses of the jurors interviewed, are also discussed.

341. Wolfgang, Marvin E. and Marc Riedel. "Rape, Race, and the Death Penalty in Georgia." AMERICAN JOURNAL OF ORTHOPSYCHIATRY, 45(4): 658-668, July 1975.

In 1972, the Supreme Court ruled that the imposition of the death penalty in cases where the victim's life was neither taken nor endangered is in violation of the eighth and fourteenth amendments to the United States Constitution, which prohibit cruel and unusual punishment. In an effort to avoid this ruling, the Georgia Legislature enacted a statute which established discretionary standards for sentencing. In this article, Wolfgang and Riedel examine this statute and the effect of race on the sentencing of sex offenders. In an effort to discover if race is a factor in the severity of sentence received by a convicted rapist, the authors analyzed the discretionary sentencing of three hundred sixty-one (361) rape cases in Georgia. They found that the most significant variable in this analysis was the racial combination of the victim and the offender, and that black defendants who raped white women were most likely to be sentenced to death for the offense.

342.   Women Against Rape. STOP RAPE. Detroit,
           Michigan: Women Against Rape, 1971.
           50 pages.

           Although this pamphlet briefly discusses
           the sociological and psychological aspects
           of rape, its focus is on rape prevention.
           Methods for preventing rape by using
           simple objects such as a comb, a pencil,
           or keys are described, and an illustrated
           section on "bodily techniques" of self-
           defense is presented.

343.   "Women Against Rape." TIME, 101: 104,
           April 23, 1973.

           This brief article deals with the development
           of rape crisis centers and anti-rape squads
           across the country. While crediting the
           Women's Liberation Movement with the
           creation and growth of rape crisis centers
           and anti-rape squads, this article mentions
           a few police departments that have set
           up special procedures for dealing with
           rape cases. The organization and operation
           of rape crisis centers in general are also
           discussed.

344.   Wood, Jim. THE RAPE OF INEZ GARCIA. New York:
           G.P. Putnam's Sons, 1976. 221 pages.

           This book centers around the controversial
           rape and murder case of Inez Garcia, a
           rape victim who had turned a gun on her
           assailants and was subsequently accused
           of pre-meditated murder. The details of
           Garcia's murder trial are related with
           sensitivity. Wood feels that the physical
           rape of Inez Garcia was only the beginning
           of her trauma. Following her trial from
           its beginning through its verdict and
           sentencing, the author emphasizes the point
           that the rape victim is twice traumatized--
           once during the actual rape, and again
           during criminal justice processing,
           especially during the trial.

345. Wood, Pamela Lakes. "The Victim in a Forcible
Rape Case: A Feminist View." AMERICAN
CRIMINAL LAW REVIEW, 11: 335-354,
Winter 1973.

The author notes that a most unusual fact
about rape cases is that the offender is
frequently treated in a sympathetic
manner, whereas the victim is met with
hostility. Rape laws do little to remedy
this situation, since the requirements of
proof for a crime of rape are more
stringent than for other crimes.
Consequently, victims are reluctant to
report the crimes because of these stringent
requirements and the prevalent myths which
make rape an impossible crime to commit,
and profess each alleged victim's complaint
as being false. Wood reviews some of the
traditional justifications for the stringent
requirements of proof for rape. These
justifications include: victim precipitation,
"female masochism," a woman's desire for
revenge on a man, and the victim's desire
to maintain a good reputation. The
issue of resistance, which is important
to a rape case, is also discussed. Wood
explores what she terms "the complainant's
ordeal," which begins when the victim
reports the crime and ends, technically,
with the verdict following the trial. Some
changes in the laws governing rape, and
alternatives to the present system for
processing a rape complaint are suggested,
and the need for emotional support for the
victim is emphasized.

346. Woods, G.D. "Some Aspects of Pack Rape in
Sydney." AUSTRALIAN AND NEW ZEALAND
JOURNAL OF CRIMINOLOGY, 2(2): 105-119,
1969.

The phenomenon of pack rape, or gang rape,
is explored with the emphasis being on
the sociological factors leading to the
commission of the act. The author states
that pack rape is part of a pattern of
sexual behavior, and not an isolated
incident. Drawing upon the theories of
sociologists such as Durkheim, Merton, and
Thrasher, Woods attempts to explain the

163

causes of pack rape with the use of probable
sociological explanations. The influence
of population density and social disorganization
are important to his analysis. Some
recommendations for reform in the procedures
for the punishment and/or treatment of rape
offenders are also suggested.

347. Younger, Irving. "The Requirement of Corroboration
in Prosecutions for Sex Offenses in New York."
FORDHAM LAW REVIEW, 40: 263-278, 1971.

The author explores the corroboration
requirement for sex offenses, emphasizing
the requirement as applied in New York
State. Corroboration requirements in states
other than New York are also discussed.
Regarding the corroboration of sex offenses
in New York State, Younger discusses the
new Penal Law, effective since September
1967, as applied to sex offenses. Methods
for improving New York State's corroboration
requirement are suggested.

348. Zuspan, Frederick P., coordinator. "Alleged
Rape: An Invitational Symposium." THE
JOURNAL OF REPRODUCTIVE MEDICINE,
12(4): 133-152, April 1974.

The participants in this symposium, with
the exception of two, are medical doctors.
The participants respond to some very
basic questions pertaining to the physical
and psychological treatment of the rape
victim. Although realizing that the actual
determination of whether a rape actually
occurred is a legal question, the physician's
role in examining the victim and taking
medical evidence to assist in determining
if a rape did occur, is discussed in detail.
The importance of having specialized
personnel for treating the rape victim in
the hospital emergency room is suggested,
for both the physical and psychological
health of the patient. Methods for the

treatment of venereal disease and the prevention of pregnancy are explained. Following a discussion of the extent of rape in this country, some methods for curtailing rape are suggested.

PERIODICAL LITERATURE REPRESENTED

Akron Law Review

Albany Law Review

American Criminal Law Review

American Journal of
Criminal Law

American Journal of Nursing

American Journal of Obstetrics
and Gynecology

American Journal of
Orthopsychiatry

American Journal of Psychiatry

American Journal of
Psychoanalysis

Annals of the New York Academy
of Sciences

Archives of Sexual Behavior

Arizona Medicine

Australian and New Zealand
Journal of Criminology

Australian Journal of Forensic
Sciences

Baylor Law Review

Big Mama Rag

Boston Globe

British Journal of Criminology

British Medical Journal

Brooklyn Law Review

California Law Review

Canadian Journal of
Corrections

Canadian Nurse

Canadian Psychiatric
Association Journal

Carolina Law

Chitty's Law Journal

Cleveland State Law Review

Columbia Law Review

Connecticut Law Review

Corrective Psychiatry and
Journal of Social Therapy

Cosmopolitan

Crime and Social Justice: A
Journal of Radical
Criminology

Criminal Law Bulletin

Criminal Law Review

Criminologist

Editorial Research Reports

Federal Probation

Fordham Law Review

Fordham Urban Law Journal

Forensic Science

George Washington Law Review

Georgia Law Review

Good Housekeeping

Harper's Bazaar

Hastings Law Journal

Hofstra Law Review

Hospital Physician

Houston Law Review

Human Behavior

Indiana Law Review

Inform

Intellect

International Journal of
Child Psychotherapy

International Journal of
Criminology and Penology

International Psychiatry
Clinics

Issues in Criminology

John Marshall Journal of
Practice and Procedure

Journal of Abnormal Psychology

Journal of Criminal Law and
Criminology

Journal of Criminal Law,
Criminology, and Police
Science

Journal of Forensic Sciences

Journal of Pastoral Care

Journal of Pediatrics

Journal of Personality and
Social Psychology

Journal of Psychiatric
Nursing and Mental Health
Services

Journal of Psychiatry and Law

Journal of Religion and Health

Journal of Reproductive
Medicine

Journal of Sex Research

Journal of Social Issues

Journal of the American
Academy of Child Psychiatry

Journal of the American
Medical Association

Journal of the American
Medical Women's Association

Journal of the Florida
Medical Association

Judicature

Ladies' Home Journal

Law and Order

Law Quarterly Review

Louisiana Law Review

Loyola Law Review

Loyola University Law Journal

McCalls

Mademoiselle

Majority Report

Manitoba Law Journal

Medical Annals of the District of Columbia

Medical Aspects of Human Sexuality

Medical Trial Technique Quarterly

Medicine, Science, and the Law

Medico-Legal Journal

Michigan Law Review

Minnesota Law Review

MS. Magazine

National Observer

Nebraska Law Review

New England Law Review

New Mexico Law Review

New Society

New York

New York Times

New York Times Magazine

New York University Law Review

Newsweek

North Carolina Law Review

Nursing Research

Obstetrics and Gynecology

Off Our Backs

Pageant

Pediatrics Clinics of North America

Pennsylvania Medicine

Pittsburgh Forum

Police Chief

Prime Time

Progressive

Prosecutor

Psychiatric Spectator

Psychology Today

Psychotherapy: Theory, Research, and Practice

Public Health Reports

Quarterly Review of the District of Columbia Nursing Association

R.N.

The Radical Therapist

Ramparts

Reader's Digest

Redbook

Resident and Staff Physician

Rocky Mountain Medical Journal

Rolling Stone

San Francisco Chronicle

Second Wave: A Magazine of the New Feminism

Seminars in Psychiatry

Sexology

Sexual Behavior

Social Problems

Social Work

Society

South Carolina Law Review

Stanford Law Review

Straight Creek Journal

Suffolk Law Review

Sweet Fire

Syracuse Law Review

Texas Law Review

Texas Medicine

Texas Tech Law Review

Time

Trial Magazine

Tulane Law Review

Tulsa Law Journal

University of British Columbia Law Review

University of Chicago Law Review

University of Cincinnati Law Review

University of Colorado Law Review

University of Florida Law Review

University of Pennsylvania Law Review

University of Richmond Law Review

Urban Review

Valor

Valparaiso University Law Review

Victimology: An International Journal

Village Voice

Virginia Law Review

Vogue

Washington and Lee Law Review

Washington Post

Washington University Law Quarterly

Washingtonian

Wayne Law Review

Western Journal of Medicine

William and Mary Law Review

Willamette Law Journal

Wisconsin Law Review

Women: A Journal of Liberation

Women Lawyers Journal

Yale Law Journal

SUBJECT INDEX

Historical perspectives: 4,12, 21,24,39,50,87,108,121,157, 185,199,248,307,311

Homosexual rape: 45,178,192, 210,306

Incest: 11,19, 204,306,339

Incidence of rape: 50,57,60,84, 85,136,142,147,148,157,182,191, 203,214,252,261,266,270,273, 274,275,276,277,279,280,284, 287,301,303,348

Intent: 68,78,152,199,228, 230,241,254,308

Interracial rape: 13,21,86,87, 341

Little, Joanne: 87,313

Location of the offense: 7,9, 120,143,144,152,176,189,199, 204,209,214,251,276,277,292

Media, influence of: 33,50, 70,93,159,222,312

Medicolegal Procedures: 58,70, 83,95,99,101,103,127,139,146, 202,216,238,272,300,309,323,329, 348

Myths concerning rape: 4,39,50, 87,104,180,187,195,205,209,255, 283,289,291,295,322,345

Non-violent rape: 21,25,126, 128,155,179,195,219,255

Offender characteristics: 7,15,50,104,120,142,152,157, 172,191,204,209,223,226,251, 263,339

Police: 2,16,17,26,30,38,52, 57,58,60,70,82,84,85,91,96, 106,113,119,139,146,150,153, 167,168,169,170,175, 176,180, 184,194,196,198,205,214,218, 237,238,245,250,252,256,260, 268,271,278,280,284,285,291, 297,300,301,317,319,325,339, 343

Pornography: 122,171,294, 304,306

Pregnancy: 5,34,109,138,146, 216,302,348

Prevention: 11, 31,33,36,37, 40,54,58,84,107,111,117,131, 136,142,146,148,156,157,160, 174,175,176,180,189,204,205, 208,213,219,227,231,246,259, 263,267,273,286,293,294,298, 300,309,319,325,328,342,348. see also self defense

Prior offense record: 6,8, 152,199,228,230,292

Psychological reactions, victim: 2,7,16,39,41,47,109, 111,112,127,133,137,175,176, 184,192,193,195,198,200,201, 204,216,216,236,238,252,256, 266,268,278,280,293,294,296, 300,309,315,317,332,340

Psychology of sex offenders: 62,64,74,84,105,110,115,120, 63,186,187,213,215,217,229, 244,247,294,303,317,320

Public education programs: 20,37,55,104,131,148,185, 227,252,299

Race: 6,8,24,28,57,86,89,139, 143,144,172,214,223,226,233, 251,271,276,277,287,325,341